Early Childhoods in a Changing World

Early Childhoods in a Changing World

Edited by Margaret M Clark
and Stanley Tucker

Trentham Books

Stoke on Trent, UK and Sterling, USA

Winner of the IPG DIVERSITY Award 2010

Trentham Books Limited

Westview House   22883 Quicksilver Drive
734 London Road   Sterling
Oakhill   VA 20166-2012
Stoke on Trent   USA
Staffordshire
England ST4 5NP

First published 2010

British Library Cataloguing-in-Publication Data
A catalogue record for this book is available from the British Library

ISBN: 978 1 85856 473 9

Designed and typeset by Trentham Books Ltd and printed in Great Britain by The Cromwell Group, Trowbridge, Wiltshire

Trentham is an ethical publisher and uses paper only from sustainable forests

Contents

Section V
Challenges and Changes • 143

Dedication

*In dedicating the book to Pamela Taylor, Principal of
Newman University College, Birmingham, from 2000 to 2009,
we acknowledge her vision which led her to encourage the
development of a range of early years courses, both full and
part-time, of which Newman is so justly proud.*

Acknowledgements

We are grateful to all the contributors for so enthusiastically co-operating in the writing of this book. In spite of their busy professional lives they have borne with us as we set deadlines and asked for changes in their Chapters to meet the overall plan of the book and to enable us to provide a book that we hope will appeal to a wide readership.

Illustrative material and experiences of families have been included in the Chapters to bring the issues alive; they also make the book enthralling reading. Though many of the stories are based on real families, we have taken care to preserve their anonymity. The exception is in Chapter 11 where members of the family have been involved in discussing their own experiences.

We are grateful to Carol Millington for her assistance in preparing the manuscript for the publisher.

Our thanks to Trentham Books for agreeing to publish the book. It has been a pleasure to work with Gillian Klein of Trentham Books who has shared the journey with us and been helpful and enthusiastic throughout.

Margaret M Clark and Stanley Tucker
December 2009

About the Authors

Anca Bejenaru is Lecturer in Social Work at the Lucian Blaga University of Sibiu, Romania. Her main field of study is social work with the child and family. Her present research interests include child adoption, violence against children, youth and women and social work in school.

Jennifer Bowes is a Professorial Fellow at the Institute of Early Childhood and Associate Dean, Research of the Faculty of Human Sciences, Macquarie University, Australia. She is also founding Director of Macquarie University's Children and Families Research Centre and has conducted research on child development and education.

Stig Broström is Associate Professor in Early Childhood Education and Care, School of Education, Arhuus University, Denmark. He has a PhD from the Danish School of Educational Studies linked to the University of California, San Diego, on the topic of learning and social development in USA and Denmark: an ethnographic study of everyday life in a Danish and American kindergarten.

Eileen Carmichael is an education consultant who recently retired from Learning and Teaching Scotland where she was responsible for the development of Early Years online and for the Early Years Matters Newsletter. She was National Development Officer in Scotland at the time of the preschool education initiative and the development of A Curriculum Framework for Children 3-5.

Margaret M Clark is Visiting Professor at Newman University College, Birmingham. She was awarded an OBE for her services to early years education. She has both a PhD and a DLitt, the latter for published work on literacy, and is a Fellow of both the British Psychological Society and the Scottish Council for Research in Education. She has an international reputation for her research in early education and literacy.

Philomena Donnelly is Director of the Postgraduate Diploma in Primary Education and lecturer in early childhood education at St Patrick's College, Dublin. Her PhD was on the topic of young children's philosophical thinking. She was one of the principal research directors for an EU-funded project on Diversity in Early Years Education, and has recently researched the experiences of immigrant families starting school in Ireland.

Johanna Einarsdottir is Professor of Early Childhood Education, University of Iceland, School of Education, Reykjavik. Her PhD in Early Childhood Education is from the University of Illinois. She has extensive experience in early childhood education and in teacher education. She is currently conducting research on early childhood teachers, children's views on their preschool education, and transition and continuity in early childhood education.

Sue Ellis is Reader in Literacy and Language Development in the Department of Childhood and Primary Studies, University of Strathclyde, Glasgow. She is interested in multidisciplinary approaches to literacy education and in effective teacher development.

Rebekah Grace is a Postdoctoral Fellow at the Children's and Families Centre, Macquarie University, Australia. She has conducted research on the experiences of children with disabilities and their families and is currently researching how low income families experience early childhood education.

Eve Gregory is Professor of Language and Culture in Education, Goldsmiths, University of London. She works with students on BA, MA and doctoral courses. Her research and publications span the areas of early years, bilingualism, literacy development and family involvement in learning and she has recently directed or co-directed projects on the role of siblings and grandparents in young children's learning.

Kerry Hodge is a Postdoctoral Fellow at the Children's and Families Centre, Macquarie University, Australia. She has explored issues in identifying giftedness in young children and is currently investigating the experiences and beliefs of early childhood teachers regarding gifted children and their families.

Mary James is Director of Little Elephant Pre-Primary School (LETCEE) in Greytown, South Africa. LETCEE provides professional training for early childhood development practitioners and implements a family-based programme for children too ill or too poor to attend school.

Foster Kholowa is Lecturer in Language and Literacy Education in the University of Malawi. He has a PhD in Education (early literacy) from the University of Malawi (and Sussex, UK). He is a specialist in early childhood development and primary education and is currently Board Chair of the Association of Preschool Playgroups in Malawi.

Dorothy McMillan is a Senior Lecturer in Early Childhood Education at Stranmillis University College, Belfast, teaching on a number of Early Childhood Studies degree programmes. Her research interests include the preschool curriculum, parental partnerships and parenting skills. The conceptual notion of educare in preschool settings and its implications for early years training was the focus for her PhD.

Joanna McPake is Vice-Dean for Knowledge Exchange, Faculty of Education, University of Strathclyde, Glasgow. Until 2009 she was Director of the Scottish Centre for Information on Languages Teaching and Senior Researcher at the University of Stirling; before that she was a Research Programme Manager at the Scottish Council for Research in Education.

Lydia Plowman is Professor in the Stirling Institute of Education and Director of Research, University of Stirling. She has previously worked as a Programme Manager at the Scottish Council for Research in Education and as a Senior Fellow in the School of Cognitive and Computing Sciences in the University of Sussex.

Horatiu Rusu is Associate Professor of Sociology at the Lucian Blaga University of Sibiu, Romania. His research interests include inter-ethnic relations and social change in post-communist societies. He was author of a book on socio-cultural identity in Romania and co-edited books on issues connected with the social transformations of Eastern European societies.

Siân Wyn Siencyn is Head of Early Years Education at Trinity College, Carmarthen. She worked in the private, statutory and voluntary sectors in Wales, specialising in early years provision and policy. Her particular area of expertise is early bilingualism and she edited the first major Welsh language publication on Early Childhood Studies. She has been involved in the new early years policy in Wales as a member of the Welsh Assembly Government's Advisory Panel on Early Years and was a member of their panel on Children's Rights.

Christine Stephen is Research Fellow at Stirling Institute of Education, University of Stirling. She is an experienced researcher with a developed interest in preschool education and young children's learning. Her research activity pays particular attention to articulating the perspectives of children, parents and practitioners. With Lydia Plowman and Joanna McPake she has conducted a number of UK research council-funded studies of young children's experiences with digital technologies.

Allison Tatton is Senior Lecturer in Early Years Studies, Newman University College, Birmingham. She is Programme Co-ordinator for the Foundation Degree for Teaching and Learning Support Assistants. In 2004 she undertook a research project into the skills gaps and training needs in the early years sector.

Stanley Tucker is a Professor and Dean of the School of Community and Professional Development at Newman University College, Birmingham. He has researched and published extensively in the area of educational and social policy and its impact on the lives of children and young people and their families.

Glenda Walsh is Principal Lecturer in Early Childhood Education, Stranmillis University College, Belfast. Her research interests and publications fall particularly into the field of quality issues and the early years curriculum. She is involved in the longitudinal evaluation of the Early Years Enriched Curriculum project, which is guiding the course for the Foundation Stage of the revised Northern Ireland curriculum and a further study in the Republic of Ireland which is examining pedagogy in early childhood education.

Lynne Williamson is Director of the Connecticut Cultural Heritage Arts Programme, a state-wide folk arts initiative at the Institute for Cultural Relations, Hartford, USA. Her work involves professional museum practice, community based oral history and technical assistance projects, arts administration, teaching and cultural conservation.

1

Introduction: Themes and Issues

Margaret M Clark and Stanley Tucker

Changing childhoods

It is almost impossible to avoid images and stories in the media about the changing nature of childhood. We live in what some people call a 'global village' (Cochrane and Pain, 2000), where it is easy to obtain instant pictures of children suffering from starvation, being caught up in the aftermath of war, or sewing shirts for pitifully low wages for large multinational companies. There is as much debate about what constitutes effective early years education and care in China as there is in Russia or the United States. Governments across the world search for panacea policies that will change the nature of childhood, eradicate poverty and improve economic effectiveness.

In this book you will encounter discussion and debate about many of these issues. You will examine real life case study material that captures the different circumstances in which children and their families find themselves. Crucially you will be asked to reflect on the issue of what it means to be a young child in twenty-first century society. In the book we do not confine ourselves to debates about childhood in the United Kingdom but challenge you to reflect on the experiences of children living in testing circumstances elsewhere in the world. We introduce you to a variety of early years policies and practices. We show how resilient children and their carers can be as they strive to improve their life chances. We argue that there is much to learn from evaluating ideas drawn out of the positive experiences of children and their families in other countries.

This book is primarily intended for students on early years programmes, both undergraduate and postgraduate and those on courses on child development and children and families. Depending on your interests you can build on the illustrative material to develop your own case studies, follow up the research reported and the references for further reading.

The book takes as its starting point the need to reflect on the diverse and changing nature of children's lives. It seeks to demonstrate how particular issues, problems and dilemmas are experienced by children and their families. The examples draw on widely different experiences in many parts of the world. Each Chapter focuses on a specific aspect or experience of early childhood, written by an author with knowledge and experience in the field of early years and working with children and their families. The names of all children and families featured have been changed to protect their anonymity, except for the family in Chapter 11 who are involved in telling their own story.

Using a thematic approach the book explores how different childhoods are shaped and influenced by both local and global perspectives. Each of the five sections is introduced by a brief outline and some key questions to consider when reading the following Chapters. The sections are divided thus:

Section I Changes and transitions

Section II The changing nature of social isolation

Section III Changing generations

Section IV Who cares?

Section V Challenges and changes

Illustrative material, questions posed and activities suggested within each Chapter encourage you to relate the issues to your own circumstances. Although there are numerous texts on childhood, this book is unique in bringing alive the experiences of such a wide range of families. The adoption of a global perspective enables you to compare and contrast the early years experience of children from different parts of the world and to compare those with children within your own experience.

Each section of the book features at least one Chapter reflecting experiences of families in a part of the United Kingdom (England, Northern Ireland, Scotland or Wales). Experiences of families living in remote rural areas and in urban areas in different parts of the world are also featured in each section. The case studies reveal just how many transitions are experienced by today's young children.

In the final Chapter we group the issues in a rather different way, encouraging and guiding you to look back at the Chapters in the light of cultural background and its impact on family life, and of family dynamics, including the role of siblings and grandparents. We also explore briefly policy and practice in early education and care, directing you to relevant Chapters in this book and elsewhere.

Overview of key themes

Key themes emerge that are common to a number of the Chapters. It is important to understand these themes as they provide the backdrop to many of the policy and practice issues explored. To gain the greatest benefit from book it is vital to reflect critically on the themes and to make connections between them and the specific arguments being developed by each author. Sometimes the themes are presented up front; at other times there may be a need to dig beneath the surface of the debate.

Different childhoods

The first of the themes challenges the idea that children who come from a particular community, town, region, culture, religion or country experience childhood in the same way. How many times do you encounter people in the media for example talking about 'young children today'? Or hear a parent agonising about their child's progress when compared to others in the same class? Or academics pronouncing on the expectations of the *normal* child? And it is easy to feel overwhelmed by statistical data that attempts to create connections between age, social class, gender, ethnicity, etc. We are not saying that such perspectives can't be helpful but we are concerned that in any attempt to really understand the needs, aspirations and experiences of an individual child or group of children you have to take a more holistic view of their development.

Bronfenbrenner (1979) for example wrote of the need to understand child development in terms of the individual, the family and the wider communities with which children engage. Crucially the idea of 'reciprocal action' is introduced for consideration where a range of different kinds of interactions and relationships have to be evaluated and understood. It is also important to understand that some children and their families may be more at risk than others; yet others may be more 'resilient' when it comes to dealing with the challenges they face (Rixon and Turney, 2007).

Factors shaping childhood

The second of our themes in many ways builds on, and expands, the points made earlier. We argue that the life chances of particular individuals and groups of children and their families are influenced by social, psychological and economic factors. The impact of poverty for example is keenly felt by many children and families across the globe. It can be a key factor in determining quality of housing, health, sanitation, educational opportunities and future life chances as well as expectancy. The experience of living in a war-torn region or country can have significant psychological and social outcomes when community and family bonds are fractured (an issue taken up in two of our case studies). However, where governments are willing to invest proactively in early years education and care, evidence suggests that the quality of life of children and families is likely to improve significantly (Hendrick, 2003).

Social construction

Our third theme takes us into more difficult conceptual territory in that we want you to read the contents of the book from a critical position. We want you to apply the ideas of 'social construction'. Essentially social constructionism is about challenging the 'realities' that we take for granted. As Stainton Rogers (2001:26), argues there is a need to deconstruct the things that we 'know about our world and how it works' and the processes of 'human meaning-making'. For many people this can be a difficult step to take. Our sense of who we are, what we know and the values we hold is to a significant extent determined by individual and collective representations of the world around us. You can, for example, see the poor as scroungers, work-shy and feckless.

Yet it is important to ask where these kind of representations come from. What evidence is there to support certain dominant representations of childhood? Ask yourself about the role the media play in deciding what constitutes good and bad parenting. Think about how children are viewed in a society where they are required to work to support the family and where the rich countries castigate such activity yet continue to buy cheap goods. We think this book will challenge you to reconsider your views and ideas. For example, Chapter 15 by Broström challenges ideas concerning social competence and the ability of young children to be involved in decision making. In part, that competence can be seen to arise out of a social construction of children that values their independence and promotes positive learning environments.

Rights and voice

Next we take up the theme of human rights, particularly as this relates to listening to the voice of the child. The United Nations Convention on the Rights of the Child (UNCRC) (UN, 1989) stands as one of the most significant landmarks in the promotion of children's rights. As Donnelly (2003:150) notes, the speed with which 'it came into force was stunning; it took less than a year to obtain the twenty required parties (in contrast to the two and a half years for the Convention against torture).' Specific issues such as nutrition, health, wellbeing and education featured strongly in the concerns of the Convention. Matters of protection from harm, the need to provide services to meet the specific requirements and demands of the young and the importance of seeing children as participating in decision making were all highlighted. Recognition of the 'evolving capacities' of the child and matters of protection against discrimination and exploitation, and the need to provide mental, spiritual and social development provided the philosophical underpinnings for the Convention.

We have encouraged contributing authors to capture the voices of children and their families through the illustrative material. We felt this was necessary because we believe such an approach is vital in truly capturing the real life difficulties, dilemmas and experiences the young encounter. An aspect of the intention of the UNCRC is to encourage the participation of children in the decisions that impact on their lives. We need to move away from *adultist* preoccupations of wanting to create a world that reflects *their* needs and aspirations (some might argue they are creating a world in their own image) and ignores the needs and aspirations of children (Dalrymple, 1995). We hope that the book makes some contribution to this particular intention of the UNCRC. In addition the authors introduce particular concepts and theories to support their arguments, some of which might be new to you and require you to undertake further reading to assess their full significance. An edited collection such as this can only provide a series of useful signposts to potentially relevant academic literature.

The message we want to leave you with here is that you read the book from a critical perspective. Think carefully about what is being said. Use the questions provided to explore key theories and debates. Weigh up the 'evidence' used by the authors as they present their ideas. Decide on the issues and debates you want to explore further. Above all we hope you enjoy the experience of reading the book.

References

Bronfenbrenner, U (1979) *The Ecology of Human Development.* Cambridge MA Harvard University Press

Cochrane, A and Pain, K (2000) A globalizing society. In Held D (ed) *A Globalizing World? Culture, economics and politics.* London Routledge.

Dalrymple, J (1995) It's not as Easy as You Think! Dilemmas and advocacy. In Dalrymple, J and Hough, J (eds) *Having a Voice: an exploration of children's rights and advocacy.* Birmingham: Venture Press

Donnelly, J (2003) *Universal Human Rights in Theory and Practice Second Edition.* New York: Cornell University Press

Hendrick, H (2003) *Child Welfare: historical dimensions, contemporary debate.* Bristol: The Policy Press

Rixon, A and Turney, D (2007) Safeguarding. In Robb, M (ed) *Youth in Context: frameworks, settings and encounters.* London: Sage.

Stainton Rogers, W (2001) Constructing childhood, constructing child concern. In Foley, P, Roche, J and Tucker, S (eds) *Children in Society Contemporary Theory and Practice.* Basingstoke: Palgrave

United Nations (1989) *Convention on the Rights of the Child.* Geneva: UN

Section I
Changes and Transitions

From an early age all children have to face many transitions. These are not only to do with proceeding through the school system, although these are the transitions on which much research focuses. Sometimes even very young children may have to adapt to very different regimes when transferring from home to preschool, to a childminder, to extended family members acting as carers, even within a single day. In Chapter 2 the expectations of parents in Iceland with regard to playschools and transition to primary school are considered. In Chapter 3 the focus is on refugee children's experiences in Ireland and those of their family, as the children move into primary school. The role of siblings and grandparents is seldom examined in terms of their potential to ease the transition of young children from home to school. In Chapter 4 this issue is considered, in particular for children in London whose culture and language differs from that of the primary school.

- Make a list of the number of transitions that children today might face before they reach the age of eight. Remember to include horizontal as well as vertical transitions.
- Consider the role expected of the parents and the ways this might differ as the children move from one setting to another.

2

Icelandic Parents' Views on Playschool Education and the Transition to Primary School

Johanna Einarsdottir

Introduction

In recent years, the concept of quality in early childhood services has been challenged and redefined. Quality is regarded as a relative concept and definitions are likely to change, according to context as well as values and beliefs of various stakeholders. This new notion for defining quality considers multiple truths and voices (eg Dahlberg and Åsén, 1994; Dahlberg *et al*, 2007). Mabry (2001), for instance, discusses how truth wears many faces: the playschool director's *truth* for instance, is not the same as a parent's or child's truth. Therefore, the varied perspectives of different stakeholder groups, such as the educational authorities, school directors, teachers, parents, educational experts, and the children themselves, should be acknowledged. Katz (1995) considers quality from the perspectives of different stakeholders. She suggests five perspectives for assessing the quality of child-care:

- top-down, the perspective of the adults in charge of the programme
- bottom-up, the perspective of the children attending the programme
- outside-inside, the perspective of the parents
- inside, the perspective of child care staff and
- outside, the perspective on how the community and the larger society are served by the programme.

This Chapter focuses on quality from the outside-inside perspective of parents, and presents results from a study on Icelandic parents' views on their children's early childhood education and transition to primary school. It begins with a short introduction to Iceland and brief overview of its history of early childhood education, including the emphasis in the National Curriculum Guidelines for Playschools.

Iceland is one of the Nordic countries, although it is distant from the other Nordic countries, located in the Atlantic Ocean midway between Europe and America. The population is approximately 319,000. Icelanders enjoy a living standard comparable to that of their European neighbours, and the welfare system resembles that of other Nordic countries. Everybody, for example, reaps the benefits of free health care, free education, and guaranteed pensions, and parents have the right to nine months paid leave for pregnancy and childcare. Icelanders work long hours, and women's participation in the labour market is high. Currently more than 90 per cent of Iceland's people live in urban areas, with approximately 32 per cent of the population in the Reykjavik metropolitan area (Hagstofa Íslands, 2009).

The Ministry of Education formulates educational policy and publishes the National Curriculum Guidelines for Playschools, which contains policy-setting guidance for pedagogical work in playschools and is meant to provide a flexible framework (Menntamálaráouneytio, 1999). The local authorities supervise and bear the cost associated with the building and operation of most playschools. According to the National Curriculum, playschools should care for children, as well as provide them with a healthy learning environment, secure play conditions, and the opportunity to participate in group work and play. Play is regarded as the foundation for children's learning and development, and should, therefore, be the central and predominant feature of children's preschool experience. The curriculum also stresses the need for children's participation in a democratic society. For instance, they should play an active role in making plans and decisions about their school day, and evaluating situations as they arise. Social competencies, such as following rules, resolving disputes peacefully, and respecting the rights of others, are also stressed. Playschools also work with subject areas such as language, movement, nature, the environment, culture and society. Each playschool develops its own educational plan.

A fundamental principle of Icelandic education is that everyone should have equal opportunities to acquire an education, irrespective of sex, economic status, residential location, religion, disability, and cultural or social background. The Icelandic educational system today is divided into four levels. Playschool is the first level, intended for children age 6 and under. Compulsory school is intended for children from 6- to 16-year-olds. Children begin compulsory school in the fall of the year they turn 6. Research in Icelandic playschools and primary schools shows evidence of discontinuity between these two early childhood settings and the curriculum guidelines represent two different tradition of teaching young children (Einarsdottir, 2006). The primary school curriculum emphasises the teaching of subjects and pupil assessment (Menntamálaráouneytio, 2006).

Children are not required to attend playschool but, according to legislation, all children must have the opportunity to do so. Attendance rates have been rising in recent years, mainly because most mothers are in the work force but also because of the increasing recognition of playschool as an important part of children's lives. Approximately 90 per cent of children aged 3 to 5, and almost all 5-year-olds, attend playschools today (Hagstofa Íslands, 2009).

The research study
Method
The study reported in this Chapter investigates parents' views on their children's playschool education and their expectations for primary school. The study was conducted in three playschools in Reykjavík in 2006. Participants were parents of 43 5- and 6-year-old children who were finishing playschool and starting primary school in the fall. The participant parents were interviewed in focus groups of four or five people and the interviews took place in the children's playschools. A focus group study is a carefully planned discussion with a selected group of individuals designed to gain information about their attitudes, opinions, and perspectives. and experiences with a particular topic (Kruger and Casey, 2000).

The focus group interviews were semi-structured. They consisted of set questions but were also open for discussion of additional topics. The interviews emphasised the parents' views of the role of playschool and its pedagogy and curriculum, as well as their children's daily life in playschool. Specific focus was placed on the children's playschool learning, the activities the parents considered important and what they were most and least satisfied with in their children's playschool experience. The parents were also asked about their expectations for primary school.

Findings

According to the *Curriculum Guidelines* (Menntamálaráouneytio, 1999), playschool education should aim at development rather than knowledge. Emphasis is placed on informal learning, play and social skills. The results of this study reflect the curriculum guidelines. In general, the parents were pleased with their children's playschool education. For them it was most important that their children were happy and lived in harmony in their playschool; the way in which the playschool day was organised and the content of the curriculum appeared less important. Happiness, from the viewpoint of most parents, meant that their children felt safe and had a positive relationship with their peers and staff in the playschool, and learned to interact and play with others. It was also important to the parents that the child's individuality should be valued, they learn self-reliance, and they manage situations independently.

All the parents reported that their children were happy in playschool, and that the development of sound friendships was the most important aspect. They agreed that if their children were allowed to enjoy themselves as individuals and play with their friends, then they were more likely to be happy. One mother commented:

The children are happy and content, and they look forward to going to playschool, and they do not want to go home. That is very good and good testimony for the playschool. It is a good place to be.

Role of playschool

When the parents were asked why their children attended playschool, many of them mentioned that their children needed a safe place to stay while their parents were working. However, they also stressed the importance of playschool as the first educational level; a significant link in their children's education where they learned important things. One of the fathers said, '[Playschool] is a preparation for life. Children will be left out if they don't go to playschool, socially and in other ways. When they come to primary school, all the other children will have attended playschool.' The parents agreed that they would have their children attend playschool even if they were not working outside the home, although they might not have them stay all day. The parents viewed playschool as an important place for children to learn to interact with other children and adults.

Social skills

Overall, the parents viewed playschool primarily as a place for their child to gain social skills. One mother said, 'I find it important that they develop socially and learn to relate to people with respect and that sort of thing and also respect their environment.'

The parents also mentioned empathy, respect, and the importance of children's putting themselves in others' shoes. One mother said:

> Naturally, interaction with other people is of vital importance. You know when children are always in playschool or in a group, they are not alone at home with their mother as it was in the old days. It is very important that they learn how to relate to other people and how other people relate to you.

Related to this is the emphasis the parents placed on their children learning to understand the perspectives and feeling of others. 'They need to learn self-respect', one mother said, 'and learn to believe in themselves. ' In a similar fashion, another mother said that it was important that the children learned to:

> hold on to their views, but at the same time to learn to respect others' views. Find some healthy balance, like you are trying to do all your life.

The parents also agreed that it was important that children gained self-confidence and belief in themselves, because, as one mother said, 'so they stand by themselves, but at the same time, respect other children'. In connection with the importance of children learning to show affection and respect for each other, parents in one of the focus groups discussed bullying as the discussion below indicates:

> Mother 1: You know, learn to respect other people.
>
> Father: Yes.
>
> Mother 2: Put themselves in others' shoes.
>
> Mother 1: Yes.
>
> R: Social development?
>
> Mother 3: Yes, exactly. And everybody can become a victim of bullying, and they can help other children [who are having a difficult time].
>
> R: Precisely.
>
> Mother 1: And respect that people are different.

This reflection on the development of social skills is consistent with recent research with Icelandic playschool directors who emphasised socialisation, informal teaching through play, and creative activities in playschools (Einarsdottir and Karlsdóttir, 2005).

Self-reliance

Promotion of self-reliance and independence was mentioned as an important aim of playschool education. Parents in one of the playschools discussed how thankful they were that the staff made the effort to help children become self-reliant. They found it important that the children were encouraged to do activities by themselves, such as dress and undress, help themselves during lunch and snack-time, and solve simple problems independently. In one group the parents discussed the importance of children learning self-reliance and managing situations by themselves, and one of the parents said:

> Take their shoes off, spread their bread, and things like that. These are things that we do not have time to teach them; we are always working and in a hurry.

In the focus group quoted below, the parents discussed what children should learn in playschool:

> Parent 1: How to function in the society, have regard for others, be able to make decisions, and be content with your decisions, be polite to other people, and, of course, be self-reliant and able to help yourself.

> Parent 2: Yes, and be honest and polite.

This is consistent with other studies that show that parents rank self-reliance as an important task to learn in preschool. Grace and Brandt (2006), for instance, found that parents regarded it as most important for later success in school that their children were able to care for personal needs and were confident and felt good about themselves and could follow directions.

Playschool personnel

The educational personnel in the playschool are key people in the lives of children and their parents. One mother said, 'A good staff with pleasant manners is most important for the children and the parents.' In most of the groups the parents mentioned the importance of good staff, and many expressed their satisfaction with the educational personnel. Many of the parents mentioned that they found it very important that the staff welcomed the children when they arrived. One mother said:

> On cold winter days it is homey; it feels good to go outside and leave your child when you know she is happy and there is someone who is taking care of her, giving her breakfast, and things like that.

The discussion below is from a focus group and develops the theme of the need to provide a welcoming environment:

> Parent 1: I am very satisfied with the staff. They are very hospitable and the playschool is so homey and not too strict.
>
> R: What do you mean by that?
>
> Parent 1: They welcome the children heartily when they arrive in the morning. Someone always comes and says, 'Good to see you,' and offers them breakfast.
>
> Parent 2: I find that the staff really enjoy the children, and are happy to see them.

A recent study on parental participation in Icelandic playschools points to the importance of parent-teacher communication when parents pick up and drop off their children (Einarsdottir and Garoarsdóttir, 2009). The results show that parent-teacher communication occurred most frequently through daily chat during drop off and pick up transition points. The results of a comparative study of German and USA parents' perceptions of their children's care show that parents in both countries ranked greeting and departing as the most important item (Cryer *et al*, 2002).

In some groups the parents were dissatisfied with not meeting the playschool teachers when they picked up the child. Below is an excerpt from a discussion in one of the groups about this:

> Father: We pick our children up late in the day. Often the staff that is there then are not the same people who have been with them during the day. Then we do not get information about how the day was. You know, did they eat well during lunch and those sorts of things.
>
> R: Exactly.
>
> Mother: If your child has recently been sick, you would want to know how he was doing during the day. Then the staff do not know [if they were not there].
>
> R: Yes.
>
> Mother: Then you have to remember to ask the next day.

This discussion is consistent with the results of the Endsley and Minish (1991) study on communication between parents and staff in day-care centres during morning and afternoon transition. Results revealed that caregivers were relatively more accessible during the morning transition, while parents were more accessible during the afternoon transition.

Play and learning

The parents were not totally in agreement about how much play and how many planned activities there should be for the oldest playschool children. Their views seemed to differ according to the playschools. In one of the playschools, the parents stressed the importance of play. One mother said, 'I think you should not push the children. They should have the opportunity to play.' And one father said, 'I think boys should be allowed to be boys. You know, within limits.' Some parents mentioned that, with age, organised group activities should be increased. Parents in this playschool also emphasised the importance of outdoor play and complained that if there were too much organised group work, this might reduce the amount of time for outdoor play. One father said:

> At one time there was a lot of emphasis on handicrafts [in this playschool]. I am sure it is good, but you shouldn't put too much emphasis on it. Children need to go outside and move.

In the second playschool, the parents complained about the programming being too strict which reduced the amount of play-time. They felt that the children should be allowed to be free to play, and the parents should be allowed to bring their child to the playschool at a time convenient for them, not necessarily for the playschool. One mother said that a teacher had complained when she brought her child in late to playschool.

In the third playschool, parents in one group discussed that the playschool should give the children the opportunity to learn more in order to prepare them for primary school. The parents also talked about the possibility of more stimulating and exciting activities for the oldest children, such as more field-trips. One parent asserted that children who were used to formal and rigid programmes and schedules in playschool were better prepared for primary school than those who had attended a playschool where there was more freedom. On the other hand, another parent stated:

> I think children need both; they need rules and schedules, but also play. If they can just do what they want to do all day, they become bored. Some children stay in playschool eight or nine hours a day, so they have to have a programme and some organised activities.

However, there were also parents in this playschool who talked about how happy they were with the homely atmosphere. They found the school building was well organised, there was ample space in the classrooms, and there were many small rooms where the children could play in small groups.

Transition to primary school

Most of the parents regarded starting primary school as a major step in their children's lives. One mother said: 'This is a completely different world'. Many of them mentioned that they expected this to be a big change for the children who have had the freedom to play and choose what to do in playschool. One of the fathers said:

> I find these transitions to be very subtle. They are extremely subtle this summer. From them being on four legs in the bathroom playing with blocks in the playschool and then suddenly they go to school where they have to sit still for 40 minutes.

These views are in agreement with the results from studies around the world. The parents in Griebel and Niesel's study (2002) considered the days of care-free childhood years were over when their children started primary school. Graue (1993) examined the views of parents in kindergarten and First Grade and found that they had very different expectations for kindergarten and First Grade. They expected kindergarten to be a social experience with some academic material shepherded by caring, nurturing teachers. They expected First Grade to be an academic experience that develops beginning reading and maths skills, directed by someone who is clear and enthusiastic.

Many of the parents were worried about how their children would manage when they started primary school. Some of the parents mentioned that the children were so small that they were not ready to start school. These attitudes are in harmony with the results from a study by Dockett and Perry (2007). The parents in their study had the feeling that their children were too young to start school and dreaded this turning point in their children's lives; they found that the preschool was safe, but the primary school was 'scary'. Pianta and Kraft-Sayre (1999) also found that the parents in their study were worried about the transition to primary school.

The parents worried about structural factors such as recess (break-time) and the size of the school buildings. They also talked about the fact that there were more adults and more supervision in the playschool and the environment was more secure. The discussion below illustrates this:

> Mother 1: ...the playschool teachers here are so many. This is so secure. They take good notice if someone is teasing him or if something is the matter with him.

> Mother 2: But in the primary school the child might be left behind and forgotten.

> Mother 1: There is perhaps just one woman who is the teacher. Then he might just be forgotten because he is just like that. He does not say: 'Hey I am here… I will just have to tell the teacher what to do.'

The parents were generally not worried about academic issues. In one of the groups the parents discussed reading and literacy education and if they should start to teach their children to read before they started school:

> Mother: I was beginning to think about what to do now. You know, this is the last playschool year. Should I start teaching him the letters of the alphabet? You know: when he comes to school he might be the one who knows the least.

> Father: We were mainly thinking. Where is he compared to the other children? Have they started to read but he has not?

These observations are congruent with the results of Graue's (1993) study with US parents who were worried about their children's standing compared to other children when they started school. In the play-based curriculum of playschools, comparisons among children are not prominent. When children start primary school they are often required to do the same things at the same time and then their strengths and weaknesses in academic subjects become more striking.

Summary and discussion

The results of the study show that, in general, parents in these Icelandic play-schools were satisfied with the emphasis on play and social skills development in their children's playschool. This accords with the analysis in the recent OECD report on early childhood education where two different approaches to curriculum were identified: the social pedagogy approach and the pre-primary approach (OECD, 2006). The social pedagogy approach is prevalent in the Nordic countries and the results of this study suggest that Icelandic parents are satisfied with the emphasis placed on broad developmental needs of young children, their wellbeing, socio-emotional development, and motivation to learn. They do not want the focus to shift to academic subjects, such as reading, writing, and mathematics, which seem to be the trend in English speaking countries.

Points for discussion

- How similar would the views of parents and practitioners in your country be to those expressed by the Icelandic parents in this Chapter?

- Contrast the 'social pedagogical approach' to early education described in this Chapter to that referred to as 'the pre-primary approach' in OECD 2006.

References

Cryer, D, Tietze, W and Wessles, H (2002) Parents' perceptions of their children's child care: a cross-national comparison. *Early Childhood Research Quarterly* 17 p259-277

Dahlberg, G and Åsén, G (1994) Evaluation and regulation: a question of empowerment. In Moss, P and Pence, A (eds), *Valuing Quality in Early Childhood Services.* London: Paul Chapman

Dahlberg, G, Moss, P and Pence, A R (2007) *Beyond Quality in Early Childhood Education and Care: languages of evaluation.* London and New York: Routledge

Dockett, S and Perry, B (2007) *Transitions to School: perceptions, expectations, experiences.* New South Wales, Australia: UNSW Press

Einarsdottir, J (2006) From pre-school to primary school: when different contexts meet. *Scandinavian Journal of Educational Research.* 50(2) p165-185

Einarsdottir, J and Garoarsdóttir, B (2009) Parental participation: Icelandic playschool teachers' views. In Papatheodorou, T and Moyles, J (eds), *Learning Together in the Early Years: exploring relational pedagogy.* London and New York: Routledge

Einarsdottir, J and Karlsdóttir, K (2005) Hvernig tala leikskólastjórar um leikskólann? *Tímarit um menntarannsóknir,* 2(1) p53-67

Endsley, R and Minish, P A (1991) Parent-staff communication in day care centers during morning and afternoon transitions. *Early Childhood Research Quarterly* 6 p119-135

Grace, D J and Brandt, M E (2006) Ready for success in kindergarten: a comparative analysis of teacher, parent, and administrator beliefs in Hawaii. *Journal of Early Childhood Research* 4(3) p223-258

Graue, E M (1993) Expectations and ideas coming to school. *Early Childhood Research Quarterly* 8 p53-75

Griebel, W and Niesel, R (2002) Co-constructing transition into kindergarten and school by children, parents and teachers. In Fabian, H and Dunlop, A-W (eds) *Transitions in the Early Years: debating continuity and progression for children in early education.* London: Falmer/Routledge

Hagstofa Íslands. (2009) Accessed June 2009 from http://www.hagstofa.is/

Katz, L G (1995) *Talks with Teachers of Young Children.* New Jersey: Ablex

Kruger, R A and Casey, M A (2000) *Focus Groups. A practical guide for applied research.* Thousand Oaks, CA: Sage

Mabry, L (2001) Representing the truth about program quality or the truth about representing program quality. In Benson, A D Hinn, D M and Lloyd, C (eds), *Visions of Quality: how evaluators define, understand and represent program quality.* Amsterdam: JAI

Menntamálaráouneytio (1999) Aoalnámskrá leikskóla [National curriculum for playschools]. Accessed May 2009 from http://bella.stjr.is/utgafur/leikskensk.pdf

Menntamálaráouneytio (2006) Aoalnámskrá grunnskóla [National Curriculum for Primary School]. Accessed May 2009 from http://bella.mrn.stjr.is/utgafur/general.pdf

OECD. (2006) *Starting Strong II: early childhood education and care.* Paris: OECD

Pianta, R C and Kraft-Sayre (1999) Parents' observations about their children's transitions to kindergarten. *Young Children* 54(3) p47-52

3

Starting School in Ireland: the experience of young children from the refugee community

Philomena Donnelly

Purpose of the Study

This Chapter reports on the findings of a two-year research study (2005-2007) into the experiences of refugee children starting primary school in Ireland. Rutter (2006) talks of the lack of research on the *educational experiences* of children who are refugees in comparison with the volume of studies on the *traumatic experience* of these children. For the Irish educational system to cope and plan Irish based research was important. Although a small scale study, this research offers an insight into how thirteen individual families with refugee status found the experience of the first two years in the Irish primary school system

In the last years of the twentieth century and in the first years of the twenty-first century Ireland experienced unprecedented economic growth sometimes referred to as 'the Celtic tiger'. With the collapse of much of Western banking in 2008-9 Ireland is one of the countries severely hit by economic recession. During the years of economic growth Ireland attracted many immigrants and those seeking asylum. At its peak in 2002 there were 11,634 asylum applications. By 2008 this had reduced to 3,866 applications.

Background

The Irish Republic has a population of 4.2 million. The majority of children start primary school at 4 years of age although the statutory age is 6. About

44,000 primary school children, representing ten per cent of the number of children attending primary school, were born outside the State (Department of Education and Science, 2009). There are 23,226 primary school children who were born in other European Union countries, and another 20,703 born outside the EU. (For further background information see Clark and Waller, 2007:83-108.)

Since April 2000 there has been a system of direct provision for people entering Ireland and claiming refugee status. Direct provision means that claimants are given full board and accommodation in a government designated centre, often run and managed for the State by private providers. Those seeking refugee status are not permitted to choose or change address nor are they allowed to work. This, it can be argued, contravenes international law. The Reception and Integration Agency is part of the Department of Justice, Equality and Law Reform (DJELR) and is responsible for implementation of Government policy on immigrants and refugees. In 2002 Ireland recognised 2,000 asylum seekers as refugees. However in 2004 Ireland introduced a constitutional referendum granting the right to Irish citizenship to children born in Ireland to non-Irish parents. The impact of this was that in 2005 the number granted refugee status had dropped to 966. In this same year, 2005, 25 per cent of people living in direct provision centres were under the age of 4 years.

Research participants

During 2004-2005 thirteen parents living in one of Ireland's largest refugee accommodation centres agreed to participate in the study. They were all women and all had a child starting primary school in September 2005. Seven of the participant children were girls and six were boys.

The research was conducted through a series of interviews with the parents and with the children in the presence of their parents. The initial interviews were conducted in August 2005, before the children started school, to determine the parents and children's perceptions and expectations of Irish schooling. The second interviews were conducted at the end of the first term in school, in December 2005, followed by the third interviews in June and July 2006 when the children had completed a full year in the primary system and then again in June and July 2007 at the completion of the two-year early years cycle of primary school (aged 4 to 6 years).

Parents gave written permission to participate in the research and the children were asked on each occasion if they wished to take part in that particular interview. On two occasions children declined, one was playing football and did not wish to be interrupted, and another child was not present in the family home.

Initially some parents showed great caution and requested that the interview would not be audio-taped but were happy for the researcher to take notes. The initial set of interviews in August 2005 took place in the families' living quarters in the accommodation centre. By the time of the second set of interviews, many of the families had been given residency status and had moved to rented accommodation outside and all were comfortable with being audio-taped. The research was funded by St. Patrick's College, Drumcondra and all of the College's ethical guidelines were adhered to. The research method was informed by the work of Clough (2002), Miller (2000) and Pollard (1996) and took a narrative approach to constructing meaning. As Miller argues:

> ...the life story is an active construction of the respondent's view of their life. There is no single 'best' or 'correct' construction. The content of a life story that a respondent will give in an interview will be dependent upon how they see their life at that particular moment and how they choose to depict that life view to the person carrying out the interview. (Miller, 2000:139)

The excerpts from the research in this Chapter give an insight into the parents', children's and a principal teacher's perception of the transition for children starting school while living in a refugee accommodation centre and then moving into residence in a community.

Profiles of the families

Twelve of the families are from Nigeria and one from Ghana. They had been resident in Ireland living in direct provision from a period of five months, the shortest time, to three years, being the longest. Some of the families had been moved from other direct provision sites to this larger site. The average wait for resident status for most families was about two and a half years. Five of the women were accompanied by their husbands with the rest having come alone with their children. One family had four children, three had three children and the rest had two children. Nine of the mothers had third level qualifications. These included a diploma in marketing, a post-graduate diploma in marketing, a higher diploma in banking and finance, diploma in accountancy, diploma in computer science, a degree in psychology, diploma in travel and tourism, diploma in food science and technology and a degree in economics. The other mothers had all attended secondary school. Of the five fathers, one had a degree in engineering, one was qualified in computer science and one was a motor mechanic.

The parents all spoke of their desire that their children would do well in school and hoped that they and their children could add value to the country by becoming educated, finding employment, and thus adding to society. Three expressed concern about possible bullying and racist remarks. They had heard talk of this possibility from other mothers who had school children. They were unsure if it was true, but it was what they feared. Their expectations were that their children would receive a good education and make something of their lives. As one mother summed it up:

> I would like my daughter to become somebody good in the future, take care of herself and make herself an asset.

One of the difficulties for the families was finding out how the Irish educational system works and how to register their child for a school place. The grapevine was the most common means of accessing information and five of the thirteen parents found a school through friends who had school children. This work seemed to fall on the shoulders of the mothers in particular. Two found a school through their church, one through a resource centre in a large near-by town and the other four were allocated schools by the Department of Justice, Equality and Law Reform. The children had all attended the preschool in the accommodation centre; parents had found this experience to be enriching and spoke very highly of it. The children began school in September 2005 while they were still resident in the accommodation centre, and a series of buses collected them in the morning and returned them in the afternoon. This caused some anxiety for the parents as they were afraid that the children might not get on the right bus or be left behind. For this reason some parents opted to collect the children themselves.

During the Autumn of 2005 many of the families received their residency papers and began the transition from the accommodation centre to living in Irish society. At the initial interview many of the parents spoke of the tension in the waiting and the wondering when it would happen. This continued for many of them throughout 2005-2006. By the end of the first school year, all except one of the families had made the transition from the accommodation centre into life in Ireland. One family was still resident in the centre in February 2008 because of complications in her case. For the other twelve children, their first term in primary education was against this back-drop of anxiety and uncertainty in their family lives. For example, there was a dilemma for some families as residency is given on an individual basis. So for one of the research families the father received his residency papers, and was therefore supposed to move immediately, while his wife did not receive hers until several months later. In this case, the mother had to stay on in the Centre with their three children while the father had to move out. This also became a cause of concern and anxiety to mothers who wished their husbands to join them from their country of origin when they had received their residency papers. Some of the children had not seen their fathers since they were small babies and had no real memory of them.

Transitions

The transition into Irish society for twelve of these children coincided with their first term or year in primary school (4- and 5-year-olds). Over half of the children had lived in two different accommodation centres and were now required to move again. Eleven of the children had to move school when their family moved out of the accommodation centre. Thus, these children had a great deal of change and upheaval to cope with while simultaneously nego-tiating school itself. The majority of the parents attended an information meeting for new parents at the various schools. Some parents had to wait until a place became available in a school. All of the parents felt comfortable approaching their child's teacher and found the schools welcoming.

Once residency is granted, applicants are no longer the concern of the DJLR. The first major hurdle for the families is to find accommodation. Again many did this through friends and indeed four of the families who were friendly in the accommodation centre all moved to the same housing estate. However, this was not always a simple task. One mother who was on her own with three young children found the search for rented housing very difficult. When her eldest child was in school, she brought the other two by bus into Dublin and through a friend eventually found accommodation in West Dublin. Then the task was to find a local school that had a place for her child. This became a crisis issue for the families and indeed for the educational system as a whole. Some schools in particular areas such as Fingal in North County Dublin and West Dublin simply could not cater for the demands being made on them. One child in the research group had started a school while in the accom-modation centre but when her family moved into residency, the local schools had no place for her and she was not in the school system until the following term. When interviewed at the end of term, December 2005 and January 2006, the majority of the families were in the middle of adjusting to living in Irish society. Many would have liked to have known more about the Irish language and Irish culture. Importantly, most said they knew little about the Irish edu-cation system.

At the same time it proved possible to reveal many positive experiences for both parents and children. For example, the parents found the primary curriculum and teaching approaches a lot more creative than they had experienced in their own countries and felt that the curriculum was closer to 'the nature of the child' with less pressure, and children doing painting and other creative activities. One comment was: 'It's all about the children, it's all about learning'. In general the children loved school and talked about playing outside and singing. The children were aware of differences between home and school, as were parents, for example 'home English' and 'school English'. This was a reference to how some Dublin children drop the 'th' sound to just 't' in words like 'thunder'. They made friends and felt a sense of belonging: ' ...one day I forgot my lunch and a white boy give me a sandwich'.

The children when interviewed gave very positive comments about their experience, with one exception. The girl who had been attending a primary school but could not find a school place when the family moved out of the accommodation centre, and was out of school for several months, found starting a new school towards the end of the first term very difficult. She complained: 'They won't play with me'.

A number of parents also expressed worries around the amount of change experienced by their children and felt the change to a new home, new area and new school was unsettling for the children. One mother made the point that once parents have residency they were allowed to work, unlike when they were living in the accommodation where they are forbidden to work. Prior to gaining residency status, children spent all of their time with parents and had become very accustomed to having them around all of the time. When parents moved out, most of the mothers were either participating in training courses or working so the children had to re-adjust to this change as well as all of the other changes. At the same time the process of transition brought with it specific challenges. One of the greatest dangers for the parents and the children is poverty. While conducting the December 2005 interviews it was apparent that having found rented accommodation many of the families could not afford heating. Children would be dressed in coats and hats at home and curtains would be drawn in an effort to keep any heat within the house.

One year later
Parents and children were interviewed again in June 2007. There was a distinct improvement in the physical well-being and energy levels of parents, mostly because the worry of obtaining residency status as well as the search

for housing and settling the children into school was over. One parent spoke of 'a wonderful, wonderful year'. The children too were much more relaxed and in their interviews gave lots of detail about their daily living, playing with toys like dinosaurs and jig-saws, playing with dolls, having fun; as might be expected, friends and birthday parties featured largely. When asked to describe themselves, one child made the following comments:

> I'm from _____ (mentioning the accommodation centre), we came from Nigeria and then we came from _____ (name of accommodation centre) and then we moved here. I remember going to school in Nigeria with my pink Barbie bag. Pink is my favourite colour.

The mothers meanwhile were completing courses, many in childcare and care of the elderly. Some were working in office administration. Their social lives tended to be confined to their respective churches and to families they had become friends with in the accommodation centre. One mother was a member of her church committee. They said they did know some Irish parents from chatting at the school gate but there was a caution around taking such friendships further. One Irish mother who took the initiative on this by asking some of the children around to play with her daughter and invited some of the children to a birthday party was mentioned by four of the mothers. She was the only Irish parent they felt they really knew. One parent felt 'up and down', largely because she was dealing with three young sons, was completing a full-time training course, her husband was having difficulty obtaining residency in Ireland and was still living in Nigeria. The GAA (Gaelic Athletic Association) came in for much praise for encouraging and involving the children in their voluntary sports activities, chiefly Irish football.

Parents did comment on the cold, wet and fog that is often part of Irish weather as a negative. They all preferred the Irish primary education system to that which they had experienced in Nigeria and Ghana. There were little items that intrigued them, for example, a mother asked what '*go maith*' (Irish for good) meant, as it was written on her child's report and she did not understand it. Parents had concerns but in general, having achieved residency status they were very positive about their families' future. As one mother put it 'you have to remember I'm living my dream'. The Ghanian mother commented on how intrigued she was that Ireland is a country where you could make a living telling jokes on television. She found it difficult to understand that this was someone's job. Many of the families are single parent; usually the mother is head of the family and is often expected to send money back to her country of origin.

To secure and continue with residency status it is compulsory that applicants are either on an education course or in paid employment. They are asked to produce this evidence after two years from being granted residency status. This regulation caused one of the mothers a great deal of worry because she was finding it impossible to find work that facilitated her leaving and collecting her eldest daughter at school. A member of her church, whom the child had not previously known, offered to take the little girl to live with her and in desperation the mother agreed. This was a distance of 100 kilometres from the child's home. By 2007 the child had returned to the family home and was attending the local school.

Another perspective

As part of understanding the experience of children starting school through the refugee process, the principal teacher of a school where five of the children attended was interviewed. The school had been opened recently and had a very active programme of parental involvement. The principal found that opportunities for parental involvement being offered by his school were only being taken up by Irish parents and some Western European parents. He had therefore initiated a number of tailored programmes to encourage other parents. He suggested there were a number of reasons for their lack of participation:

- the parents of non-EU children were exceedingly busy and did not have the time to get involved with the school
- there can be a feeling that some African parents are over differential and do not think it is their place to be involved in school. Unlike Irish parents they do not come up to complain
- confidence is also a factor because of their own perception that they do not know enough about the education system and
- many of the children could by the end of their second year of primary education have attended two, three or even four schools
- the energy to establish a relationship with a school takes time so they may think they are not going to expend that energy when they are so insecure with their own lives.

In recent times with the economic downturn, the Irish government has initiated new rules from June 1st 2009 that require employers to double the length of time for which a vacancy is advertised before hiring a non EEA person (the EEA comprises the EU as well as Norway, Liechtenstein and Iceland but excludes Romania and Bulgaria) (*Irish Times* 16/4/09). Although this new ruling should only apply to new migrant workers it may very well impact on non-EEA residents applying for jobs. Permits will no longer be issued for low-paid jobs, domestic workers and truck drivers. Despite qualifications, migrant workers, sometimes because of language issues, often end up in low paid employment. There is also the danger with unemployment rising steeply that unless political leaders take the initiative racism could become a greater issue. Already some Irish parents are moving their children from schools with high numbers of immigrant children to country schools or other schools with a lesser concentration of immigrant children. The principal interviewed as part of this research had such experiences:

> we had our new junior infants class in last Friday week and we have lost three out of nine white children since then and undoubtedly when I talked to all three it was to do with their children were going to be a minority in the school.

One other major issue for this principal was how to handle what he called 'critical multi-culturalism'. He felt that there is a need in Irish education for a radical approach to engaging in a dialogue with parents around concepts of childhood and not to avoid dealing with issues such as attitudes to corporal punishment. Indeed in the interviews a Nigerian mother asked why Irish parents 'beg' their children. She could not understand how in supermarkets she would hear Irish parents saying, 'please, please do not touch that'. Equally, Irish teachers have expressed dismay at seeing some parents hit their children. Another difference that arose during the interviews was the shock of some parents at having a male teacher for young children in the first years of primary school. This in reality is a rare occurrence in Irish primary schools as men are a minority in primary teaching, as is common in many countries.

Conclusion

The purpose of this two year research was to learn about the Irish asylum process from the perspective of participants with a particular focus on children starting primary school. Ireland is one of only two of the twenty-seven member states which have opted out of the EU Reception Directive. This Directive provides for minimum conditions for asylum seekers, including the right to work after waiting for a year for a decision on status. Becoming a refugee in Ireland is a demanding and often long process. As can be seen from this small scale research, young children are part of this process and therefore the educational needs of these children have to be part of any provision. In adjusting to life and school in Ireland, it is equally important that those already living in the country learn to readjust also. One clear outcome of the research is that parents of refugee children need help, advice and information about the Irish education system. All of the thirteen participant parents in the research are now living and working or studying and their children are all settled in school. It has been a long and demanding journey for these families and some of the children by 6 years of age had attended four schools in two different countries. Such experiences need to be acknowledged.

There are lessons for teacher education. Parents continually mentioned that they wanted their children to be seen as individuals rather than be grouped as 'newcomers', 'Nigerians' etc. It is essential that teachers understand the background to the daily lives of children living in refugee families and the transitions from asylum seeker to resident. Equally, student teachers need to learn and experience during teaching practice the school policies that facilitate immigrant children and their families' access to the education system. Case studies are always helpful in assisting student teachers to empathise with the children they will meet. Early childhood educators continuously advocate the use of story as a pedagogical approach to teaching and learning. Hearing the individual stories of children and their families, the dilemmas and issues they encountered as they negotiated their child's entrance into primary school in Ireland can assist teachers and student teachers to be aware of the human reality behind national and school policies.

Points for discussion

- What is a refugee and what is current government policy in your country on refugees?

- What aspects of the background of the refugee families discussed in this Chapter enabled them to be resilient in face of the traumas they were facing?

- What issues do you think could be particular to children from the refugee community starting primary school? And how could primary schools help to ease this transition?

References

Clark, M M and Waller, T (eds) (2007) *Early Childhood Education and Care: policy and practice.* London: Sage

Clough, P (2002) *Narratives and Fictions in Education Research.* Buckingham: Open University Press

Department for Education and Science (2009) www.education.ie Accessed April 2009

Miller, R L (2000) *Researching Life Stories and Family Histories.* London: Sage

Pollard, A (1996) *The Social World of Children's Learning: case studies of pupils from four to seven.* London: Cassell

Rutter, J (2006) *Refugee Children in the UK.* Maidenhead: Open University Press

Websites

The Irish Times www.irishtimes.com Accessed April 2009

www.education.ie Accessed April 2009

www.irishrefugeecouncil.ie Accessed August 2009

www.immigrantcouncil.ie Accessed April 2009)

www.into.ie Accessed April 2009

4

The Role of Siblings and Grandparents in the Lives of New Londoners

Eve Gregory

Introduction

Parents have long been recognised as highly influential in young children's language, literacy and learning development. Grandparents and siblings, however, have remained largely invisible from the research scene. Yet most of us will have a story, or, indeed, many stories about learning with our siblings or grandparents. This is hardly surprising. Recent statistics report that in the United Kingdom 25 per cent of grandparents are engaged in child care activities, and those who are manage to clock up a remarkable average of 15.9 hours per week (Age Concern, 2004). Tellingly, grandparents are referred to in the above report as providing the glue that binds a family together, a metaphor that neatly sums up the hidden yet crucially important nature of their help.

Similarly, the role of siblings in teaching and learning from each other is often taken for granted. Western mothers may often refer to their children as 'bickering' rather than learning together. Yet, both in traditional societies (Rogoff, 2003) and in situations where families have recently migrated, siblings can play a vital role as mediators of language and literacy in young children's lives (Gregory, 2008). Thus, an examination of what takes place between both these groups is important for both researchers and practitioners in school. Using a variety of families as illustration, this Chapter sets out to explore the nature of teaching and learning with siblings and grandparents in families who have migrated to Britain from Bangladesh and whose children attend East London schools. The Chapter first describes the setting and context in which the families live and learn, then provides short vignettes of children's learning activities. Finally, it raises questions for both researchers and teachers to consider in their future work.

Setting and context

The families whose lives we share in this Chapter live in the east London borough of Tower Hamlets. The borough directly abuts the City of London, with its skyscrapers, banks and luxury apartments, surrounding the historic Tower of London and its striking neighbour, Tower Bridge. Yet in spite of this, Tower Hamlets presents a very different picture. Until the eighteenth century, its poor and often destitute inhabitants were held outside the City by one of the City gates (Aldgate) and, from this time, the area became home to migrants seeking shelter from persecution or poverty abroad. During the eighteenth century, Protestant Huguenots escaped from France, set up their silk weaving businesses and then moved on, leaving their houses and some street names (eg Fournier Street) behind. Their place was taken by Jews seeking shelter from the pogroms in Eastern Europe in the nineteenth century. They similarly set up tailoring and other businesses, then moved on to more affluent parts of the capital in the mid-twentieth century, leaving behind not only street names (eg Adler Street), but also synagogues and a famous school (Jews' Free School).

Since the late 1970s, and in greater numbers during 1980s and 1990s, a new wave of immigrants began arriving in Tower Hamlets from Bangladesh. This time, it was not religious persecution but poverty and the desire for a better life for their families that fuelled their exodus from Sylhet, in the north-eastern corner of Bangladesh. Many of their children are now second or even third generation immigrants, whose stronger language is English; some, however, are still leaving Bangladesh to join families established in the United Kingdom. In some families both parents will have been brought up, possibly born in the UK; in others, one parent may have been brought up in the UK, the other in Bangladesh, coming as a future spouse to an established British Bangladeshi husband or wife. Thus, the children will speak either English, Sylheti/Bengali or a mixture of both at home. Whichever language is given priority, strong emotional links are retained with Bangladesh. Most families speak Sylheti, a strong regional dialect, which no longer has a written form. However, children will learn to read and write in standard Bengali which requires the learning of a new lexis and grammatical forms. As Muslims, they are united in faith and the mosque remains a centre for both religious and cultural activities; many families arrange for their children to attend classes to learn both classical Arabic for reading the Qur'an and standard Bengali.

At the start of the twenty-first century, Tower Hamlets remains one of the most economically deprived boroughs in the UK. Statistics tell us that the population grew by 35,000 between the census dates of 1991 and 2001 and that 30 per cent of the whole population was born outside Britain or Europe. However, these statistics mask the fact that the borough is divided into the largely white inhabitants in the south and the Asian residents in the north. Indeed these new Londoners account for the fact that the population is one of the youngest in the country with 28.4 per cent under the age of 19. Of these, 76 per cent is from a minority ethnic group (Office of National Statistics, 2006) and in some schools, 90 to 95 per cent or more pupils will speak a language other than English with different family members at home. This presents both challenges and opportunities to the children's teachers. Although increasing slowly, the number of teachers who share the children's language and culture is still low. The monolingual teachers are often unaware of the breadth and scope of children's multilingual language and literacy practices at home, but equally unaware of the power of English in the children's lives. All of the above contributes to the very special role played by both siblings and grandparents in young children's lives. This is illustrated through the examples below.

Siblings as skilled teachers of language and literacy

The sibling dyads we meet in this section were audio-recorded during the mid 1990s at a time when immigration of wives to join their husbands who were already living in the UK was still relatively recent. Most women spoke only Sylheti/Bengali with the result that many young children, although born in Britain, entered school speaking very limited English. It was also at a time when children were learning to read at school mainly through a *Real Books* approach (the use of good storybooks that had not been produced explicitly to teach reading). These were regularly sent home to be read by the parents to their children. After initial despair that our 6-year-olds would be unable to benefit at all from this parental programme since their parents were often unable to read the books, our researcher, Nasima Rashid, discovered a contrasting but highly skilled approach to teaching by the older siblings. Instead of reading a whole text that they could not understand to the children, the older siblings, aged from 8 to 18, all provided a firm scaffold of support as the young children learned to pronounce, internalise and read a text simultaneously. According to the level of the child, the support looked as follows:

Stage One: Strategy One: Listen and Repeat (for children at a very early stage in literacy and English learning). These interactions were typified by word-for-word repetition, sometimes over hundreds of turns, until the young child was confident enough to add one or two words herself. Here is 6-year-old Uzma with Shima, her 8-year-old sibling, reading a Meg and Mog book:

	Child	Sibling
12		gave
13	gave	
14		her
15	her	
16		fishy
17	fishy	
18		gifts
19	gifts	

Later, she repeated longer chunks where she sometimes managed only telegraphic speech (underlined denotes repeat):

	Child	Sibling
28		Peace at last
29	<u>Peace</u> in <u>last</u>	
30		The hour
31	<u>The hour</u>	
32		was late
33	<u>was late</u>	
34		Mr Bear was tired
35	<u>was tired</u>	
36		So they all went to bed
37	<u>all went</u>	
38		to bed
39	<u>to bed</u>	

As a child became more proficient, an echoing of the older sibling's words takes place, that is saying the word one second later. Here is 6-year-old Henna reading with her 12-year-old brother:

Strategy 2: Tandem Reading (bold speech denotes echoing)

	Child	Sibling
6		The postman
7	**The postman**	
8		It was Tum's birthday

9	***was... birthday***	
10		*Ram made*
11		*him a birthday card*
12	***him a birthday card***	
13		*I want to eat something*
14	***I want to eat something***	

Stage Two is marked by a child's independent reading. Nevertheless, the firm scaffolding continues. The pattern during this stage was that the sibling began reading and the child continued; reading the next one, two or three words until help was needed again. Then the sibling read the next word and the pattern recurred. The length of text read by the child gradually increased until the child read almost independently. Only *after* the child became a proficient reader did the sibling focus on meaning. This was exactly the opposite of the teacher in school where meaning preceded actually being able to read the text.

To summarise, the older sibling's support had the following features:

sustaining a fast-flowing pace; providing a firm scaffold which was only very gradually removed

expecting a high level of accuracy after the early stages which was reinforced by frequent, though not constant correction of the child

allowing the child to repeat a correction before continuing with reading

a lack of evaluative comment (eg 'good girl' etc) and explicit modelling but a complete lack of questioning during the reading of the text.

In fact, such support bears a strong resemblance to that offered by middle-class English monolingual mothers with much younger children. Crucially, the siblings never asked the child to run before being able to walk. Their reading *lessons* allowed young children to repeat accurate pronunciation many times thus fixing not only how to say a word but how to read it too, and how to gain confidence through the process. Such skill has not been formally learned but, we must assume, is imbibed by the older siblings both through observation of the young child and through their own experience of learning themselves in the new country. Such skills are, indeed, admirable.

Grandparents as teachers and learners

Five-year-old Sumayah lives with her paternal grandparents, her parents, her baby sister, one of her aunts, her father's older brother, his wife and their two children, two teenage uncles, and one teenage first cousin, *cousin brother,* whose mother died when he was a baby and who is looked after by the whole family. Sumayah and her other cousin brother, who is the same age and in the same class, are particularly close and call each other *real* brothers and sisters. This extended family shares a house which they own on a fairly new housing estate in Tower Hamlets, backing onto a canal. The house is always busy and the front door is open most of the time with people coming in and out. The family is very close-knit; the grandparents are the focal point and play an important role in all that goes on in the family. The grandmother is constantly busy, from showing her daughter-in-law how to bath a newborn baby to babysitting the grandchildren whilst their parents are occupied with work and household chores.

One of Sumayah's first comments in her interview was:

> I like to grow trees with Bubu and Dada (her grandmother and grandfather), like to go outside with both of them.

In a scrapbook she made with her grandmother she chose to include leaves from the garden, reflecting the importance of gardening in her interactions with her grandparents. She carefully identified each leaf and indicated the role of each grandparent working in the garden with her: 'This is leaf from apple tree my dada (*grandfather*) made' and 'This is leaf from chilli tree my dadi (*grandmother*) made'. Sumayah also recorded the everyday work of looking after the garden area; one page consisted of leaves with the comment: 'Me and my cousin brother help my dada and dadi clean the garden'.

Learning with her grandmother in the garden

Sumayah and her cousin brother of the same age were video-recorded working in the back garden with their grandmother. Two researchers, themselves Bengali-speaking, were with them, together with Sumayah's mother. The garden itself was relatively small and mostly paved. However, around the edges, a great variety of fruit and vegetables were growing, some placed in pots on the paving.

Sumayah first helped her grandmother collect up some vegetation which was lying on the paving. She offered to hold a carrier bag so that her grandmother, who was squatting on the ground, could put the leaves inside. Sumayah's mother suggested she should sweep the paving, which she began to do with a broom, helped by her grandmother. Sumayah's cousin brother then arrived with a full watering can and the children took it in turns to water the fruit trees and several small plants in pots. The water ran out and Sumayah offered to refill the can. Meanwhile, the grandmother removed clothes from the washing line, putting them over her grandson's shoulder, and they took them inside. When Sumayah returned with the watering can, she and her cousin watered the plants with their grandmother, each placing their hands close together to hold the can. During the activity, Sumayah talked with her grandmother and cousin about what they were doing, responded to questions from her mother about the trees and plants and made her own comments.

Throughout the activity, Sumayah's grandmother skilfully promoted a collaborative learning environment. Below we see some of the skills and knowledge Sumayah displays, fostered by the loving relationship with her grandmother:

- *Identifying plants*: for example, various fruit trees, including apples, pears and lemons. She also mentions 'tomato trees, pumpkin trees and potato trees' showing a developing knowledge of the vegetable garden!
- *Understanding conditions of growth*: for example, realising that plants need regular water to grow and that watering should be performed carefully using the watering can, giving neither too much nor too little
- *Finding out about stages of plant growth*: Sumayah is able to monitor the growth of different plants and is well aware that seeds become seedlings which will slowly grow given the right conditions
- *Knowing how colour and size change with growth*: Sumayah realises that leaves also start tiny and slowly grow and that fruit gradually changes colour as it ripens
- *Caring for the garden and feeling a sense of ownership*: Sumayah helps her grandmother to sweep up leaves in the garden using a broom. Each member of the family has different plants and trees to care for and Sumayah is particularly aware of this responsibility, commenting on film, 'this one is auntie's, this one sister's and this one uncle's'.

Sumayah's grandmother promotes a collaborative learning environment, mediating between the two children, encouraging them to act jointly as gardeners and maintaining their focus on the task in hand.

Discussion and relevance for practitioners

The two episodes presented above show how siblings and grandparents are excellent *teachers* of language and literacy, especially in families of migrant origin. In different ways, they each play a special role in developing young children's skills and knowledge. Older siblings have unique access to the content of school literacy lessons, as well as understanding the methods used by teachers in the mainstream school. Other examples collected during our research show how, during play school socio-dramatic play, siblings acted out exactly the contents and methods of the classroom. Older siblings seem to know the exact stage reached by the younger child and are able to pitch their tuition at just the right level to extend this, in ways not accessible to the parent generation or even teachers in school. In some respects, grandmothers take the opposite role from siblings in migrant families' homes. They have considerable 'funds of knowledge' of the children's heritage language, as well as knowledge of religious and other cultural practices important for the young child's developing identities (Gonzalez *et al*, 2005; Gregory *et al*, 2004). Unlike many parents, they also have the time and patience to devote to young children. In many ways, the relationship between siblings and grandparents and young children is synergistic, since all are learning from each other as they set about tasks (Gregory, 2008).

There are many ways that teachers might draw upon the strengths of both siblings and grandparents. First, they can find out about activities already taking place. Children might keep diaries about what they do with their siblings or tape their play to share with the rest of the class. Reading, games and other activities for siblings to work on together might be provided.

A survey might be conducted to find out about activities in which grandparents are engaged involving young children. They might be invited into school to share a skill, stories, their heritage language or dual language materials with the children. They might also keep scrapbooks with young children on home activities, such as those in Sumayah's family, which can be periodically shared with the class. Importantly, both grandparents and siblings should be seen as important resources; they might well have more time and inclination than parents to share their activities with teachers and schools.

NB The data presented here is drawn from a large data bank from three studies funded by the Economic and Social Research Council. These children participated in the first study, 'family literacy history and children's learning strategies at home and at school'. The intense interaction between siblings had not been predicted.

Points for discussion

- What different 'funds of knowledge' might grandparents and siblings have and in what ways might these differ from parents and teachers?

- Can you envisage difficulties if grandparents have different ideas from teachers on what 'counts' as valid knowledge and methods of learning?

- How might older siblings learn from younger children as well as vice versa?

References

Age Concern (2004) *Footsteps: learn about older people. Cross-curricular citizenship resource pack.* London: Policy Unit www.ageconcern.org.uk Accessed September 2009

Gonzalez, N, Moll, L C and Amanti, C (2005) *Funds of Knowledge: theorising practices in households, communities and classrooms.* Hillsdale, NJ: Erlbaum Associates

Gregory, E (2008) *Learning to Read in a New Language: making sense of words and worlds.* London: Sage

Gregory, E, Long, S and Volk, D (2004) *Many Pathways to Literacy: young children learning with siblings, grandparents, peers and communities.* London: Routledge

Office of National Statistics (2006) *Key Population and Vital Statistics 2004.* London: Palgrave Macmillan

Rogoff, B (2003) *The Cultural Nature of Human Development.* New York: Oxford University Press

Section II
The Changing Nature
of Social Isolation

The four Chapters in this section explore the isolation of children and their families, be it geographical or social, in different parts of the world. Chapter 5 considers the problems faced by families with young children living in remote areas in rural Wales. Chapter 6, set in Australia, highlights issues surrounding attempts to integrate young children who are developmentally different into early childhood education settings. Illustrations are drawn from families with a child who has intellectual disabilities and from a frequently ignored group of children: those who are gifted.

In Chapter 7 we move to a very different rural community, in Malawi, which is one of the poorest countries in the world. It is also among the countries most seriously affected by HIV/AIDS. Not only do the rural communities face isolation, lack of facilities and poverty, but many families also have to cope with the devastating effects of AIDS in terms of long term ill-health and bereavement. Chapter 8 is set in an isolated community in South Africa, another country devastated by AIDS and where most families face poverty, unemployment and multiple bereavements. Many young women find themselves becoming head of the family and coping with the fear of and stigma attached to a diagnosis of AIDS.

- Before reading these Chapters make a list of the possible advantages and disadvantages of living in a rural community.

- How would you define social isolation?

- Were you expected to provide facilities for young children who are gifted, who have learning difficulties, or who have been diagnosed as suffering from HIV/AIDS, what would be your first concerns?

5

The Challenges for Children Experiencing Rural Poverty in Wales

Siân Wyn Siencyn

Introduction

It is generally accepted that there is little to be gained from a discussion of childhood, as if childhood were one universally agreed, chronologically delineated experience. The terms 'multiple childhoods' and 'multiplicity of childhoods' have become common (Dalhberg and Moss, 2005), reflecting the differences in children's experiences. These differences are individual, social, linguistic and economic and are governed by the complex political and cultural forces which impact on children's lives.

As elsewhere, children's lives in Wales have changed and are changing. The impact of the establishment of the Welsh Assembly in 1999 has driven many of those changes. The Foundation Phase 3-7 years, the early years curriculum in Wales, is a radical departure from the previous approaches to early learning. Children's well-being is at its core and learning through play for all children from 3-7 years is its underpinning principle. Another important entitlement in the Foundation Phase is the role of the Welsh language. Welsh language development is now an area of learning for all children, giving them the right to become bilingual in the official languages of Wales, Welsh and English.

Wales is a small country in the west of the British Isles with a population of just under three million. Of the total population, some nineteen per cent is under the age of 19 years. The population of Wales is mainly located around the urban centres of *Caerdydd* (Cardiff) in the south east and *Wrecsam* (Wrexham) in the north east.

As in other areas of the United Kingdom, the population profile is shifting and these demographic changes have important messages for planners. The child population of Wales is falling: for example, the age group 0-4 years has seen a decline from almost 191,750 in 1991 to 163,680 in 2007 whilst the age group 5-9 years has seen a similar decline of some 20,000 (http://www.statistics.gov.uk).

A consistent downfall in the number of children, particularly in the groups under 10 years, has implications for a range of services. There will, for example, be a smaller school population and this is already resulting, in Wales, in the training of fewer teachers and in teacher unemployment or re-deployment. Some areas of Wales are already seeing a decrease in private daycare due, in the main, to fewer takers. What is perceived as expensive pro-vision, not easily accessible, less well paid work are all factors that impact on the viability of childcare.

Many of the Welsh Assembly Government (WAG) initiatives relating to children share the same underpinning principles as those of other countries of the UK. The same challenges face all: safeguarding and protecting children, ensuring good learning experiences for all children, eliminating poverty and its dire consequences for children. The WAG *National Service Framework for Children, Young People and Maternity Service* (NSF) was launched in 2005 with the aim of improving quality and equity of services, in a partnership between health, social care, education, housing, leisure, the voluntary sector together with parents, carers, children and young people. In line with almost all the WAG's initiatives for children, the NSF is rooted in the 42 Articles of the UN Convention on the Rights of the Child (United Nations, 1989) and the Assembly's seven core aims for children and young people all relating to a flying start, access to learning, to play, to leisure and culture, physical, mental, social and emotional health (including the right to respect and a voice, and to be safe).

This Chapter will focus on one major area of policy commitment which has challenged the Government of Wales and one of its core aims which is to ensure that children are not disadvantaged by poverty.

Child poverty in Wales

The Welsh Assembly Government (WAG) has, from its establishment, committed itself to the UN Convention on the Rights of the Child. Indeed, Wales was the first country in the UK to appoint a Children's Commissioner in March 2001. It is in the spirit of that commitment to children's rights that, for the first time, in the UK, comprehensive statistics on expenditure on children has been released. In 2006-7 the WAG allocated some £4.4 billion of its budget to children in Wales, which is something in the region of 28 per cent of its total expenditure. Furthermore, annual public expenditure per child is increasing. In 2005-6 some £5,600 was spent on every child in Wales and the projected expenditure per child in Wales in 2010-11 is £7,100. (Source:http://wales.gov. uk/topics/childrenyoungpeople/newsitems/budget children/?lang=en)

In her statement, releasing these statistics, Jane Hutt, the Children's Minister said:

> We have made it our goal to eradicate child poverty by 2020. By making signi-
> ficant financial investments in children's lives, ensuring they have the rights
> which they deserve, we can help make this goal a reality. (from above web
> reference, no page given)

There are major threats to this ambitious goal, not least amongst them is the impact of the economic recession. Higher levels of unemployment are leading to rises in the benefits budget and will inevitably make huge demands on the public purse. It is a concern that, when governments face economic crises, children are in danger of bearing the brunt of stringent belt tightening.

The eradication of child poverty is a major challenge in Wales. Although Wales has seen a reduction in child poverty, indeed, the fastest reduction in any country of the UK, over the past few years, that rate of reduction seems to have halted. It is increasingly difficult for policies and services to attack deeply entrenched poverty in some areas or that some families face. The link between child poverty and low educational achievement is long established. Egan (2007) outlines a number of innovative education policies the WAG has developed in order to combat the discriminatory impact of poverty on children's learning prospects, including *Flying Start* and *Free Breakfast Clubs*.

A Fair Future for our Children (WAG, 2005) launched in February 2005, outlined the WAG's programme for meeting its commitment to halve child poverty by 2010 and eradicate it by 2020.

In February 2008, Save the Children and the Bevan Foundation published *Children in Severe Child Poverty in Wales: an agenda for action* (Save the Children, 2008) presenting the findings of an investigation into the lives of children living in the most severe poverty in Wales. The report states that whilst the WAG has 'demonstrated a commitment to tackling child poverty with a child poverty strategy (2005), an implementation plan (2006)...' (Save the Children, 2008:4) the challenges are daunting. The report itself makes sobering reading:

- over one in ten children in Wales live in severe poverty where household incomes are below 50 per cent median
- there is a strong link between severe child poverty and living in a household where no adult works
- a third of children in severe poverty have a disabled parent
- there is a strong association between severe child poverty and living in a lone parent household
- factors associated with severe child poverty include: living in a large family; living in an Asian or Asian British family; living in a family where mothers do not have any educational qualifications

The report states clearly that:

> the links between household characteristics and severe child poverty are complex with many of the factors overlapping, making it especially hard for such families to leave poverty.(Save the Children, 2008:2)

This kind of research has provided the WAG with compelling evidence on which to act further. On 2 March 2009, the Children and Families (Wales) Measure, which aims to tackle child poverty and strengthen support for families in need, was laid before the National Assembly for Wales. This places a duty on Welsh Ministers to develop a new Child Poverty Strategy for Wales, which will be reviewed regularly with the goal of eradicating child poverty by 2020. In June 2009, the Joseph Rowntree Foundation published *What is Needed to End Child Poverty in Wales?* reiterating the figure of approximately 32 per cent of children in Wales living in poverty. (Winkler, 2009)

Defining poverty

One traditional way of defining poverty, prevalent in the early twentieth century, was in terms of physical needs that were either not met or were inadequate: food, shelter, clothing and so on. As standards of living improved and the welfare state became more established, this absolutist approach became, over time, less relevant. By the 1970s, Townsend (1979) proposed a concept of 'relative poverty'. He argued that poverty was:

> ....the lack of resources to obtain the types of diet, participate in the activities and have the living conditions and amenities which are customary...in societies to which (people) belong. (Townsend, 1979:31)

Current thinking on definitions of poverty, as proposed by New Labour governments, the European Commission and anti-poverty organisations, use methodologies based on official statistics on income levels. Families living in poverty are defined as those with incomes of less than 60 per cent of the national median income level (Milbourne and Hughes, 2005:4).

Contemporary discourses on poverty are often complex and relate to philosophical and political debates around social exclusion and the more practical challenges of promoting social inclusion. Walker and Walker (1997) describe social exclusion as:

> a dynamic process of being shut out, fully or partially, from any of the social, economic, political or cultural systems which determine the social integration of a person in society. (1997:8)

Whatever approach is taken, there is general consensus that poverty excludes people, and children in particular, from accessing services, resources, income, from power, and from choices in their own lives.

Rural poverty

The WAG's public policies and services for young children and families are provided through a number of key initiatives such as *Flying Start* and *Integrated Children's Centres*. These initiatives target the most disadvantaged communities in specific geographical areas, areas with high concentrations of communities and people living with complex disadvantages. This results in services being increasingly centralised. This can, in many ways, lead to more effective services: cost effectiveness and resource effectiveness. But this can be disadvantageous for people living in rural communities. There is evidence, disturbing but not surprising, that families with children with disabilities have difficulty in accessing appropriate services and this is made even more challenging when they are families with low incomes (Sharpe, 2003).

Children living in rural areas can have particularly difficult experiences. Rural poverty is not, of course, new and it is often not as evident as urban poverty. In a government enquiry into women and children in agricultural employment in *Ceredigion* (Cardiganshire) in 1865, the following evidence was given by one David Jenkins:

> I am an agricultural labourer and can speak only a little English. My wages are 1s 6d a day all the year round ... I have six children ... None of them can read or write. There is no school in the parish where I live, and if there was I could not afford to send my children to it. I never get meat except now and then a bit of bacon. I live upon potatoes, bread and cheese. The labour of children becomes valuable after 10 ... Children are useful in tending cattle, weeding, etc. Education is a good thing, but bread is better. (*Report on the Employment of Children, Young Persons and Women in Agriculture* (1870:130)

Although rural and urban poverty share many common experiences such as stigma and social exclusion, there are other unique features experienced by children living in poverty in rural areas. Akhtar (2008) outlines some of them such as: access, transport, employment and education, social networks and clubs, and housing.

Access to facilities, services and goods

As well as the financial barriers to accessing services there are also the physical factors in reaching out to services – services that may not, of course, even exist. It can often be difficult, for example, to access play, leisure and sport facilities. Additional challenges include being able to access a range of health services, including health centres, dentists and clinics. There are also limited community Internet facilities, libraries and access to home entertainment, such as digital television. Broadband and mobile phone connections are often very restricted.

Accessing goods is also a challenge, not only financially but also physically. Small rural shops are closing and when they are accessible, they are often more expensive and offer limited choice. Affordable clothes shops are located in towns or in out-of-town shopping centres.

Transport

The lack of public transport remains a key concern for children and young people in rural areas, with infrequent and costly bus services the sole option particularly for those without a family car. The cost and time involved in catching two buses to make an appointment or to access a short break service for a disabled child can prove particularly challenging. It is important to remember, also, that families do not necessarily live in villages. Many will live on isolated farms and smallholdings some miles from the nearest village. Children and young people regularly report that transport, or lack of it, is important to them as it restricts both their social and learning opportunities.

Employment and higher education opportunities

There are specific challenges in maintaining rural communities where there is a large emigration from rural to urban areas of young people seeking job or education opportunities, which may not be accessible locally. Transport issues are again key.

After school activities

Many children rely on school transport to and from school and this raises particular challenges in terms of attending after school clubs and activities arranged by the school.

Travelling to school

Many children travel significant distances each day to and from school, and this can be a particular concern for infant school age children and children who attend special schools. Travelling long distances for long periods of time daily can impact on the health and wellbeing of a child.

Sustaining friendships

Children may live some distance from each other, given the large catchment areas for many rural schools, and this makes it difficult to meet outside school hours.

Housing and Homelessness

It has been well documented that there is an acute lack of affordable housing, private rented stock and social housing in many rural areas, which is forcing many young people to leave their area of birth.

Positive impact of rural living

There are, of course, positive benefits for children who live in rural communities. *Children in Wales* reports that children in rural areas feel safer; there is space for play outdoors with no adult interference (*Children in Wales*, 2008). Even with all the social and economic pressures, there are still strong feelings of community and there are informal networks of community support. Small rural schools often act as a community focus and parents can become involved in organising fund raising events which can be powerful promoters of social cohesion. These small schools can also be democratic in nature as all children in the community attend. There is not always an evident social hierarchy. The duality of the leafy suburb versus the inner city schools is not usually prevalent in a rural community. Furthermore, in many areas, these small schools are important learning centres offering the wider community use, for example, of up-to-date computer suites. Young farmers' clubs are often vibrant and inclusive places and there are opportunities for promoting Welsh cultural and language activities such as the Urdd and its sports and other activities (www.urdd.org).

Initiatives and projects

There are examples, throughout Wales, of new initiatives and longer term services that work well in rural communities. *Mudiad Ysgolion Meithrin* (www.mym.org) has a well established network of *cylchoedd meithrin and cylchoedd Ti a Fi* (Welsh medium playgroups and parent and carer toddler groups) serving rural communities. They will often have informal transport arrangements whereby parents or carers will pick up other users. Most counties have mobile services such as toy libraries and play services which are often delivered in specifically adapted buses.

Conwy County in the rural north has established a bilingual telephone support line for parents of young children who may be facing difficulties with parenting. It is particularly suited to rural areas as it is accessible and free. Parents can talk at a time that suits them; there is no need to travel or make childcare arrangements. Users of this service are primarily from low-income and rurally isolated areas. Three Action for Children (*Gweithredu dros Blant Cymru*) social care practitioners deliver the service and, after an initial assessment, an action plan is drawn up and weekly calls are made for around twelve weeks. The *Ynys Môn* Rural Family Service, which is run by Barnardo's, targets services, people and communities who may not show up in deprivation profiles as the numbers are so small. The Family Service brings together a multi-disciplinary team, working as outreach services in rural communities.

In rural Carmarthenshire, a network of family centres has been developed and a mobile service is provided by a specially adapted bus. There is a dedicated rural worker who provides parenting education through the medium of Welsh. She makes home visits and runs groups in small, isolated villages. However, she reports a common challenge – parents living in poverty will often not take up a service as it is perceived as being stigmatising.

The following two case studies outline some of the challenges facing children experiencing rural poverty. Llinos and Josh's stories are uniquely their own but they are also, in many ways, common experiences. They demonstrate the challenges faced by many children and their families living in rural areas.

Case study: Llinos (4 years)

Llinos lives with her older brother Aled (7 years) and younger brother Sion (2 years) in a local housing association house in west Wales. Her father used to work in the local cheese factory until it closed a year ago. He was offered another job, with the same company, in the north of England. He tried it for four months but the cost of travelling and lodging away from home made it difficult. Llinos's mother works during the holidays, cleaning in a holiday caravan complex which is ten miles away. She has not worked much since Sion was born. She is feeling a little down and has seen the doctor who has given her anti-depressants. Aled has a language delay and some speech difficulties which require him to attend a Speech and Language Therapy Clinic in a town some sixteen miles away. The clinic is open there on the first Wednesday of every month. There is a bus on Thursday mornings through the village where Llinos and her family live. Llinos started part-time in the local village school, the term after her third birthday. Her mother has to take the three children to school by 9 am and then return to pick Llinos up by 12.00, back again by 3.30 pm to pick up Aled.

After Sion was born, the health visitor suggested that the family receive support from the local Home Start group. A Home Start volunteer came once a week for a couple of months. Llinos's mother enjoyed that; someone to talk to, to take Aled to school, to help play with Llinos. But Home Start has been in financial trouble since its core funding was cut. The local paper said it was something to do with National Lottery money going to the London Olympics.

The village post office closed last year, which has put a strain on the viability of the village shop. Although there is a supply of fruit and vegetables, these are not always very fresh. Family meals are not regularly set at table and the children snack on crisps in front of the television. Aled has been to the dentist once, Llinos has never been.

Case study: Josh (9 years)

Josh lives with his mother and sister Lauren (7 years) in a private rented house in a small village in mid Wales. The house is not in good condition and two of the bedrooms are damp. Josh and Lauren share a room and their mother sleeps in the living room. She is a single parent on income support. Josh's grandmother bought him a second hand computer for his birthday but they cannot get broadband in the village. The landline phone was disconnected as the rental was expensive. You have to walk half a mile, up a country road, to get a mobile phone signal.

Josh enjoys taking part in the school *eisteddfod* activities. He is in the *band taro* (percussion band) and his modern dance group won second prize throughout Wales in the *Urdd Eisteddfod*. His teacher thinks he has a real talent and has suggested that he joins a dance and theatre club but that is held on Thursday evenings at the theatre which is almost fifteen miles away. She has offered to give him a lift there but there will be no way for him to come back home.

A new afterschool club has just opened in the school and Josh's mother volunteers there and is enjoying it. Josh is giving his mother ICT lessons on the school computers.

In conclusion

Developing and funding services for children and families, by the Welsh Assembly Government are often targeted by indicators of deprivation and driven by numbers. This is neither an easy nor often an appropriate model for rural areas. Children living in poverty in rural areas are not counted and, too often, not seen. They can be hidden in affluent areas.

Services in rural areas, often delivered through the voluntary sector and funded through specific streams such as *Flying Start* and *Communities First*, can take longer to set up and to staff. The pressure of time for short term funding projects is great. The costs are, of course, greater. Transport, travel, staff time and so on strain project and service budgets. Mobile services make an important contribution, but buses are expensive to buy and to maintain.

In June 2009, the Joseph Rowntree Foundation published a report on child poverty in Wales, outlining complex and integrated steps the WAG needs to take in order to reach the 2020 target of eradicating child poverty (Winkler, 2009). The report's recommendations include: improving childcare provision, promoting flexible and good quality employment, improving the skills and qualifications of adults. The Welsh Assembly Government has much to do by 2020.

Points for discussion

■ What are the differences between the poverty experienced by David Jenkins' children in 1876 and that of the children discussed in this Chapter?

■ In what ways might it be possible to improve the life chances of children living in rural poverty? Consider the range of services involved.

References

Akhtar, L (2008) Response to Welsh Assembly Government Rural Development Sub-Committee RDC (3) p5. Cardiff: 6 March 2008

Children in Wales (2008) *Families not Areas Suffer Rural Disadvantage: support for rural families in Wales.* Cardiff: Children in Wales

Dahlberg, G and Moss, P (2005) *Ethics and Politics in Early Childhood Education.* London: RoutledgeFalmer

Egan, D (2007) *Combating Child Poverty in Wales: are effective education strategies in place?* York: Joseph Rowntree Foundation

Milbourne, P and Hughes, R (2005) *Poverty and Social Exclusion in Rural Wales.* Research Report 6. Aberystwyth: Wales Rural Observatory

Report of the Commissioners on the Employment of Children, Young Persons and Women in Agriculture (1870) Parliamentary Papers, XII p130

Save the Children (2008) *Children in Severe Poverty in Wales: an agenda for action.* Cardiff: Save the Children.

Sharpe, T (2003) *The Good Life? The impact of rural poverty on family life in Wales.* Cardiff: NCH

Townsend, P (1979) *Poverty in the United Kingdom.* London: Penguin

United Nations (1989) *Convention on the Rights of the Child.* Geneva: United Nations

Walker, A and Walker, C (1997) *Britain Divided: the growth of social exclusion in the 1980s and 1990s.* London: CPAG

Welsh Assembly Government (2005) *A Fair Future for our Children.* Cardiff: Welsh Assembly Government

Winkler, V (2009) *What is Needed to End Child Poverty in Wales?* York: Joseph Rowntree Foundation

Websites

http://www.statistics.gov.uk Accessed March 2009

http://wales.gov.uk/topics/childrenyoungpeople/newsitems/budgetchildren/?lang=en Accessed March 2009

http://www.childpovertysolutions.org.uk/ Accessed March 2009

http://www.childreninwales.org.uk Accessed March 2009

http://www.childcom.org.uk/ is the website for the Children's Commissioner for Wales. Accessed March 2009

www.urdd.org is the website for Children's and Young People's Welsh Language Youth Organisation. Accessed March 2009

www.mym.org is the website for the Association of Welsh Medium Playgroups and Nurseries. Accessed March 2009

6

Isolation and Inclusion in Australian Early Childhood Settings

Jennifer Bowes, Kerry Hodge
and Rebekah Grace

Introduction

In many developed countries, including the United Kingdom and Australia, there has been a recent policy focus on social inclusion. The term social inclusion has been used to frame broad social policies related to the participation in society and its institutions of all citizens, particularly the multiply disadvantaged (Hayes *et al*, 2008). While the terms social inclusion and social exclusion are used widely, they have rarely been applied to discussions about children and their early childhood educational experience (Vinson, 2008).

The purpose of this Chapter is to examine how social inclusion has been applied in early childhood educational settings in Australia, specifically in relation to children who are developmentally different. Inclusion policies have been developed for children with intellectual and physical disabilities and have been in place across the educational sector for more than a decade. While attention has been paid within the educational system to the experiences of children with disabilities, there has been less discussion about the social inclusion of young children at the other end of the spectrum, those who are intellectually gifted.

The negative effects of social isolation on children's development have been widely documented. Children can become lonely, alienated, develop low self-esteem, lose motivation and become depressed when they are isolated from others (Fegan and Bowes, 2009). Social isolation can stem from a number of factors other than geographical distance from others. Poverty, unemployment, low levels of education, speaking a different language, illness and disability and other forms of difference can all have the effect of isolating people from their community and preventing them from having access to the benefits of social engagement with others and their social capital (Fegan and Bowes, 2009).

Within the education system, despite inclusion policies, children can find themselves socially isolated because they are different in some way. In this Chapter we look at two kinds of children who are different from the developmental norm: children with intellectual disabilities and children who are intellectually gifted. The focus is on how such children can be included more effectively in the early years of education so that the full social and educational benefits of their community are available to them. As Hayes *et al*, (2008) have noted, one of the central insights of the work on social exclusion and inclusion has been that interventions need to take into account the needs of particular groups within the context of particular countries.

Nutbrown and Clough (2006) have widened the discussion of inclusion and exclusion of children with special needs into a broad discussion of inclusion for all children in early childhood education. They define inclusion as 'the drive towards maximal participation in and minimal exclusion from early years settings, from schools and from society' (p3). Their discussion of good inclusive practice in early childhood education goes beyond the teacher and the classroom to include parents, health and other practitioners and the community.

Early childhood education in Australia

Before considering the case of children with intellectual gifts and disabilities in more detail, it is important to give some context about education in the early childhood years in Australia. Australia has a national government with responsibility for education as well as six state and two territory governments, each of which has a separate education system with its own policies and curriculum, although there is an increasing nationalisation of assessment and curriculum. Independent (private) and Catholic schools also exist and a small minority of children are home-schooled. The age at which children start school varies across Australia, although in all states children must be in school by age 6. At the prior-to-school level, there is a diversity of providers including state or local governments, for-profit businesses, religious or not-for-profit organisations and charities.

Children with intellectual disabilities

The term intellectual disability is used to refer to impairment and limitation of cognitive skills to a mild, moderate or severe degree. It encompasses a range of different diagnostic categories including Autism, Down's Syndrome, Fetal Alcohol Syndrome and Global Developmental Delay. The notion of disability is very much driven by context and the demands of society. For example, a little boy growing up in a remote Aboriginal community may not have thought that he was different from other children until he started school and was told there that he had a learning disability. He was *disabled* because of his inability to perform according to the standards of the school environment.

Particularly over the last ten years in Australia there has been an increasing push from parents and policy makers towards the full inclusion of children with disabilities in the education system (McRae, 1996). Many Australian children with disabilities attend mainstream early childhood and school settings and participate in mainstream classes, often with the assistance of a teacher's aide. However, many children with disabilities still attend special schools or satellite classes located in the grounds of a mainstream school.

Within Australia and internationally, the journey towards the inclusion of children with disabilities has not been smooth. Parents may struggle with feeling that their child is unwelcome in both early childhood and school settings (Grace *et al*, 2008). They may be frustrated that they must constantly advocate for the rights of their child and feel that there are many obstacles to productive communication with their child's teachers (Prezant and Marshak, 2006).

While pre-service teacher education in most states of Australia must include at least some training related to working with children with disabilities, we know that many teachers see inclusion as hard work and feel inadequately prepared (Kemp, 2003). Children often struggle to find acceptance from their peers and this difficulty increases with age (McIntyre *et al*, 2006). Children may also become frustrated with feeling that the focus is always on what they can't do rather than on what they can do (Prezant and Marshak, 2006).

The inclusion of children with disabilities is certainly an area where it is possible to see wide gaps between policy and practice. Preschool and school rooms remain, for some children, very lonely and isolated places.

Gifted children

In Australia there is widespread acceptance of Gagné's (2003) developmental definition of a gifted child as one whose natural abilities are exceptional in one or more developmental domains eg intellectual. An intellectually gifted child becomes a talented older person with exceptional skills in a valued field only when that child is motivated, develops good work habits and self-esteem and when his or her abilities are nurtured by the family and educational settings.

Young Australians with advanced intellectual development are usually educated in mixed ability settings. In some states, special classes in comprehensive or selective schools exist for some gifted children aged ten years or older. In the preschool years and in the early years of primary school, separate classes for gifted children are quite rare.

A recent government inquiry into the education of gifted children identified negative attitudes to intellectual giftedness in Australia compared with attitudes to individuals who are exceptional in sport or the arts (Commonwealth of Australia, 2001). Included among the recommendations from this inquiry was more professional development for teachers since pre-service teacher training in gifted education was found to be limited or non-existent. As a result, the government has funded a computer-based professional development package distributed to all Australian schools addressing identification of giftedness and curriculum differentiation. For staff in prior-to-school settings, both pre-service training and on-the-job professional development in gifted education remains minimal. As a result, young gifted children in Australia may find themselves in classes taught by teachers who have varied and perhaps limited knowledge and skills relating to their education.

Inclusion for children who are developmentally different

It can be seen that children who have intellectual disabilities or who are intellectually gifted are generally included in mainstream educational services in Australia. However, simply being in a class of other children the same age does not necessarily lead to inclusion. As illustrated in the following vignettes, children can be socially isolated in classrooms where they are different from other children unless the teacher intervenes in some way to ensure that the child has social contact with other children and is included in classroom activities. Teachers need a range of strategies to make this happen.

The examples below of children in the early childhood years who either have an intellectual disability or are gifted are real children observed in the course of the authors' teaching or research; names and some other details have been changed to protect their identity.

A child with an intellectual disability at preschool

David was a bright-eyed 4-year-old boy with a mild intellectual disability and a significant hearing impairment. He could only hear loud voices and loud noises. David had attended the local long-day care centre since he was 2 years old. While he loved being with the other children, his enthusiasm was not always shared by his teachers. David had a passion for Rugby League. He talked loudly and constantly (and at times incoherently) about the last game he had watched. He also loved to re-enact the tries that were scored and would throw himself at the other children to demonstrate a tackle.

As a result, the other children were confused by David and a little frightened of him. The teachers had been frustrated by his very loud voice and his struggle to keep quiet when others were speaking. One teacher spoke of falling off her chair when David crash-tackled her during story time. David's parents were frustrated. They worried that the teachers were focusing on David's weaknesses and overlooking his happy nature and athletic ability. They were concerned that the teachers were not doing enough to accommodate David's hearing impairment.

The situation improved markedly when a new teacher, Tom, came to work at the centre. Tom took an interest in David and thought about how to capitalise on his strengths. He made it a habit to take note of the rugby scores each weekend so that he could engage with David on this topic. He taught the whole class to play touch football and reminded David that he could only tag those children who had agreed to be part of the game. Tom also found that making a time-out sign was the best way to communicate to David that he needed to stop talking and start listening. Tom was careful to ensure that his instructions were loud and clear and checked with David privately that he understood them. David's learning and friendships improved significantly.

A child with an intellectual disability at school

Katie felt passionately that her son, James, should attend the same school as the rest of her children. James was autistic with a moderate intellectual disability. He was able to understand basic instructions and communicate in simple, short sentences but was resistant to any eye-contact or touching. The principal was initially very concerned that the school would not be able to meet James' needs. However, he agreed to trial James' inclusion because of the existing relationship with the family and the willingness of the teacher to include James in her classroom. The school worked closely with Katie and secured government funding so that a teacher's aide could be employed to be in the classroom for four days a week. The aide not only played a supportive role for James but also conducted activities with the rest of the class so that the teacher was available to work one-on-one with James for regular periods each week.

Another very important person in the successful inclusion of James was a little girl called Abigail. Abigail could see that things were hard for James and she wanted to help him. She invited him to play with her group of friends every day. James smiled every time he was asked and always responded to her invitation with a 'Yes', even though he mostly chose to sit on the sidelines with his head down. Abigail also prompted James when it was time to line up or collect his lunch. This show of compassion and friendship from Abigail was a key to establishing widespread acceptance of James amongst his classmates. To quote 5-year-old Abigail, 'James is just James! I don't mind that he's different!'

A gifted child in preschool

Four-year-old George hovered around the childcare teacher and her assistant, preferring to talk to them rather than to the other 4- and 5-year-olds. Dinosaurs, about which he knew a great deal, were the topic of his artwork and many of his conversations. The other children soon lost interest. The adults, busy attending to children across a range of abilities, chatted with him when they could. They also tried to include him in the play and activities of the other children but he showed no interest. In music or story group times, George participated when required but he rarely seemed truly engaged. While recognising that he was very able intellectually, George's teacher worried that his poor social skills were causing him to be isolated from the other children. She had a chat with his mother, who revealed that she helped him to build models of dinosaurs and make movies about them at home, but she didn't expect that the childcare teachers would do this.

After several months another 4-year-old, Hannah, was enrolled. George was immediately drawn to her. To his teacher's amazement, George took Hannah under his wing, showed her around the playroom and playground, explained the rules and told her the names of the children. Each day they played well together and not always about dinosaurs. Sometimes George led the play and at other times he followed Hannah's lead. Their play was complex and imaginative and involved much articulate negotiation. The teacher was delighted to see George so engaged and considerate with another child.

A gifted child at school

Before she started school, Sophie insisted on learning to read at home and was soon writing sentences as well. After a visit to her prospective school, Sophie's parents worried that their daughter's academic skills were already beyond those of children who had been in school for almost a year. Cautiously, they investigated the option of skipping the first school grade. The school principal was initially dismissive but agreed after a psycho-educational assessment report indicated that Sophie was highly gifted and that her academic achievement levels matched those of the most able children in the higher grade.

Her first school term was difficult as Sophie realised the older children not only had formed friendship groups but also knew some things that she didn't know. Her academic excellence continued and she gradually settled but she told her parents that she had no friends. In the playground she often sat alone. She knew her interests were different from those of the other children, so when the teacher invited children to share their favourite books with the class Sophie declined to take her beloved *Abridged Tales of Shakespeare*, telling her parents, 'They wouldn't be interested in that!' Nevertheless, after her father spoke to the teacher, Sophie did share a brief summary of the tale she loved best and created for the classroom wall a poster showing the complexities of its characters and plot.

Discussion on children with disabilities in early childhood settings

David and James experienced social isolation primarily because it was hard for their peers to understand the motivations behind their behaviours. While to David tackling another child was part of his play, to another child it felt more like a surprise attack. For James, just being invited to play was as much social contact as he wanted. To many of the other children, his inability to engage socially and his desire to play on his own seemed strange and difficult to understand.

All of the children other than Abigail had given up including James in their play. Abigail played a very important role in breaking down peer rejection and her example demonstrates the power of peer modeling. Abigail was a popular and capable student. It is probable that only a well-liked child would hold the social capital necessary to alter the general class perception of one student.

David's story illustrates the importance of a creative and thoughtful teacher. Before Tom arrived to teach at the early childhood centre, the staff felt frustrated by David and saw him as a disruption to the group. Tom thought about how to draw on David's interests and use those interests to teach him how to interact more positively with other children. Tom also sought to understand David's learning and hearing limitations and to develop strategies that would reduce their impact on his classroom participation and learning.

A great resource in any learning environment is a teacher who takes a personal interest in all of the children and has the creativity and flexibility to incorporate their interests and acknowledge their talents. Centre directors and school principals have an important role to play in supporting the inclusion of children with disabilities and in empowering teachers to take a creative and strengths-based approach in their teaching.

Being the parent of a child with a disability presents many challenges, not least of which are the challenges surrounding communication and negotiation with service professionals, including teachers. The relationship between parents and teachers can be very different for parents of children with disabilities, especially if they feel that they must advocate for the rights and needs of their child. Feeling the need to advocate implies that there is conflict, no matter how subtle. As a result, parent-professional interactions are sometimes characterised by defensiveness and talking at cross-purposes. The meaningful inclusion of children and their families requires that both parents and teachers base their communication on a desire to understand the perspectives of the other so that they can work together in the best interests of the child concerned.

Discussion on gifted children in early childhood settings
Because of their intellectual maturity, gifted children like George and Sophie tend to think and behave like older children (Sankar-DeLeeuw, 2004) and this is what lies behind their social isolation. They don't really fit in with their age peers although they may pretend to do so in order to feel they belong. If they are gregarious, they may be sought out for their good ideas or solutions to problems. They can, however, tire of the less sophisticated interests, shorter concentration spans and less complex play of other children. If they are more introverted or find little in common, as in George's case, other children may largely ignore them. Sensing their difference, gifted children often long for a friend more like themselves, an intellectual peer, and Hannah's arrival offered George the social and intellectual connection he had been missing. Sophie was not so lucky. Even among children a year older she could not find someone who was like-minded.

Gifted children do not necessarily become productive and fulfilled adults (Freeman, 2001). Teachers play an important role in nurturing gifted children's exceptional abilities and helping them to be engaged and happy in their schooling. In a gifted child's class, sometimes the only other person whose thinking and conversation are on a similar level is the teacher. Of course, teachers have a responsibility to all the children in their care and cannot devote large amounts of attention to one child. They need strategies for changing the environment to facilitate the engagement of gifted children with other children.

Although teachers cannot always find another gifted child to be a friend, they may be able to facilitate small group experiences that offer some intellectual challenge. Sophie benefited from such an initiative. If George's teacher had incorporated his interest in dinosaurs into the classroom activities, he may have been less isolated. The teacher would need, however, to take into account the depth of his knowledge and plan appropriately as well as providing ways in which other children might participate at a level satisfying to them.

Parents worry about their gifted children and want them to be happy and accepted for who they are. They have to decide which educational setting will best suit their child (if choices are available), how much to negotiate with teachers regarding their child's needs and perhaps even whether their child should skip a grade (Hodge, 2009). Parents of gifted children need information and perhaps the opportunity to connect with other parents facing similar issues.

Teachers' role in inclusion of children who are developmentally different

Early childhood teachers need to develop children's social and emotional skills and understanding along with their intellectual and physical skills, responding creatively to all children in their care. The classroom climate is very important, and young children take their cue from the teacher's attitudes, words and actions towards individual children. Teacher tolerance of individual differences sets the tone for the class. Part of the teacher's task is to become familiar with the characteristics of developmentally different children and to understand that their own behaviour can lead to social isolation for these children. Teachers can help all children to realise that everyone has strengths and weaknesses and to develop an appreciation for diversity that includes children with differing levels of ability.

Points for discussion

■ Think of a situation where you felt socially isolated as a young child. Were you able to overcome this and, if so, what helped to make you feel included?

■ What strategies can early childhood educators use to achieve effective inclusion of children who are developmentally different?

References

Commonwealth of Australia (2001) The Report of the Senate Employment, Workplace relations, Small Business and Education Resources Committee on *The Education of Gifted Children*. Canberra, Australia: Commonwealth Government Printing Service. Accessed June 2009

Fegan, M and Bowes, J M (2009) Isolation in rural, remote and urban communities. In Bowes, J M and Grace, R (eds) *Children, Families and Communities: contexts and consequences*, 3rd edition. Melbourne: Oxford University Press

Freeman, J (2001) *Gifted Children Grown Up*. London: David Fulton

Gagné, F Y (2003) Transforming gifts into talents: the DMGT as a developmental theory. In Colangelo, N and Davis, G A (eds) *Handbook of Gifted Education*.3rd edition. Boston, MA: Allyn and Bacon

Grace, R, Llewellyn, G, Wedgwood, N, Fenech, M and McConnell, D (2008). Far from ideal: everyday experiences of mother and early childhood professionals negotiating an inclusive early childhood experience in the Australian context. *Topics in Early Childhood Special Education* 28(1) p18-30

Hayes, A Gray, M and Edwards, B (2008) *Social inclusion: origins, concepts and key themes*. Canberra: Commonwealth of Australia. Accessed July 2009 at http://www.socialinclusion.gov.au/Documents/PMC%20AIFS%20report.pdf

Hodge, K (2009) When to start school if a child's development is very advanced. *Early Links*, 13(1), 13-26. Accessed July 2009 at http://www.musec.mq.edu.au/downloads/Early_Links_13_1.pdf

Kemp, C R (2003) Investigating the transition of young children with intellectual disabilities to mainstream classes: an Australian perspective. *International Journal of Disability, Development and Education* 50(4) p403-433

McIntyre, L L, Blacher, J and Baker, B L (2006) The transition to school: adaptation in young children with and without intellectual disability. *Journal of Intellectual Disability Research* 50(5) p349-361

McRae, D (1996) *Integration/inclusion Feasibility Study*. Sydney: NSW Department of School Education

Nutbrown, C and Clough, P (2006) *Inclusion in the Early Years*. London: Sage Publications

Prezant, F P and Marshak, L (2006) Helpful actions seen through the eyes of parents of children with disabilities. *Disability and Society* 21(1) p31-45

Sankar-DeLeeuw, N (2004). Case studies of gifted kindergarten children: profiles of promise. *Roeper Review* 26(4) p192-207

Vinson, T (2008) *Social inclusion: Social inclusion and early childhood development*. Canberra: Commonwealth of Australia. Accessed July 2009 at http://www.socialinclusion.gov.au/Documents/3EarlyChildhood.pdf

7

Growing up in Rural Malawi: dilemmas of childhood

Foster Kholowa and Sue Ellis

Introduction and context

Rural Malawi is a place where families are generally poor. In this Chapter we discuss childhood development in a typical Malawian rural setting, focusing on the overall challenges facing families with young children, and we look at how families are coping. Such challenges involve social structures, community involvement, preparation for schooling, and home versus school literacy and numeracy development for children. We argue that unless these key issues are addressed, rural children will continue to face dilemmas in their development and, in the long run, this will limit their future opportunities for personal development and participation in the social and economic development of Malawi.

The socio-economic status of Malawi

Predominantly agriculture-based, Malawi is among the sixteen poorest countries of the world, with 63.3 per cent of the population living in dire poverty according to the 1998 Integrated Household Survey (GoM, 2002). Generally, poverty is more prevalent in the rural than the urban areas, where about 91 per cent of Malawi's population is said to live (NSO, 2002). Poverty is therefore a critical ingredient in understanding the situation of children and families in Malawi, as well as the context of early childhood service provision.

Malawi is among the countries most seriously affected by the HIV/AIDS pandemic. The official prevalence rate among adults (15-49 years) as reported by the Malawi National AIDS Commission (NAC) is at 12-17 per cent. This means that about 700,000 to one million Malawians in the economically productive age group were infected with HIV at the time of the sentinel surveillance of 2003. An increase in the number of orphans in Malawi is one of the most serious consequences of AIDS deaths of men and women in their prime child-bearing ages. It is estimated that there are over 800,000 orphans in Malawi, 40 per cent due to death of their parents through AIDS. Also another 30,000 children are vulnerable mainly because of the sickness of one or both of their parents, who are therefore not able to care for them properly (NAC, 2003).

Malawi uses an 8-4-4 system, that is, eight years of primary, four years of secondary and four years of tertiary education. The official age range for primary schooling is 6 to 13 years. Preschooling and adult education are considered to be part of non-formal education. The Malawi DHS Education data survey of 2002 indicates that fewer than ten per cent of primary school going children (6-14 years) attended preschool before starting primary school, spending an average of 1.7 years in preschool. In urban areas, 39 per cent of such children attended nursery school before starting primary school while only six per cent of the children in rural areas did so (NSO, 2003). This raises important questions on the extent to which children growing up in Malawi, and especially in rural areas, are being given a fair start in life both at home and school, in view of the difficult circumstances in which they grow and develop, including the adverse poverty levels and limited educational opportunities before formal schooling.

Context of childhood development in Malawi

Malawi's approach to policy and implementation emphasises holistic development of the child and therefore the involvement of a wide range of stakeholders according to the 2003 national policy on Early Childhood Development (ECD). This is premised on the fact that such an approach has countless socio-economic benefits for children, adults, communities, and society in general (Pence, 2004). Early Childhood Development stakeholders in Malawi include government ministries, development partners such as UNICEF, and local non-governmental organisations or institutions. However, there are still daunting challenges to coordinating the various implementing stakeholders to achieve a synergised implementation process for holistic development of children (Chalamanda, 2004).

Overall goals of early childhood development in Malawi

The overall goal for ECD in Malawi is to enhance the provision of quality early learning and stimulation services to all children in Malawi (MoWCD-UNICEF, 2006). Strategically, this involves issues of access, school readiness and transition to school, linkages, advocacy on ECD, parents' education, monitoring and evaluation.

Malawi uses two approaches to providing early childhood development services: the first strategy is ECD Centres, which include preschools, nursery schools, crèches, day care centres, and playgroups. The second approach, *Community Based Childcare Centres* (*CBCC*), is informal ECD or rural or village preschool care where communities take an active role in the initiation, establishment and implementation or management of the CBCC centres. Often, CBCCs are characterised by poor facilities and infrastructure, and use of volunteer caregivers with low education and training. Most financial and material support to ECD in Malawi is from international organisations, while government provides very little budgetary support for this, despite the existence of a policy and implementation strategy for ECD.

The concept of CBCC as an approach to early childhood development raises interesting issues about equity in the provision of preschool or ECD services between the urban and rural contexts. Research has shown that even within the CBCC context of ECD provision, many children are left out as only a handful are able to attend even these low quality care centres (Munthali *et al*, 2007). Low education levels of caregivers raises the question of the extent to which they may consciously engage the children in experiences that would allow them to develop adequate key skills in early literacy and numeracy. Given that young children need more attention at this stage, caregivers might not effectively address all individual children's other needs as is assumed in the policy.

Current efforts and developments to promote ECD in Malawi

Despite these challenges there are, however, inroads being made in ECD through the development of a number of policy and supporting documents for the implementation of ECD in Malawi. These include the five year National ECD Strategic and Implementation Plan ECD Training Manual, Community Based-Child Care (CBCC) guide, Parenting Education Manual, Advocacy and Communication Strategy for ECD, among others. While such documentation is commendable, there are still a lot of disparities between what is happening at national level in terms of policy and strategy on the one hand, and the realities on the ground in terms of implementation of such plans on the other. This still leaves the child in a disadvantaged position in terms of care and development, with rural areas being the most affected.

Realities around childhoods from a case study of a rural family

In this section we discuss typical realities of the childhood environment in Malawi by using a case study of one of the families, the Lukani family, and their daughter, Chikondi, from a rural community in Zomba. This community in Traditional Authority Mwambo is about eight to ten kilometres to the South East of Zomba town centre, and is generally poor socio-economically, with most of the community members living below the poverty line. A CBCC within the community acts as a focal point for community development activities including provision of early childhood development services for children, water, voluntary counselling and testing (VCT), and growth monitoring, among others. The impact of HIV and AIDS is critical in understanding the situation of families in this community.

The story of the Mrs Lukani and her family

We meet Mrs Lukani at the only CBCC in the community. She has a daughter, Chikondi, who attends the CBCC. However, Mrs Lukani has come to the CBCC on this day for a particular reason. She says she has been divorced for three years and is therefore heading a family of five, with her two daughters and two sons. She says she is HIV positive and often frequents the CBCC to get counselling, nutritious food and painkillers to alleviate her situation. We learn that Mrs Lukani is among the six to ten families that often come to the CBCC for these services. She told us her story with a great deal of emotion.

She says there are many divorces in this community. When she was expecting Chikondi, she used to go to the nearest clinic in the area for antenatal services, where she was encouraged to undergo HIV testing as a pregnant mother. She accepted and the results were shocking to her: she was HIV-positive. She was in a dilemma about whether to disclose this to her husband. When she did he was angry and decided to divorce her. His perception was that his wife must have been unfaithful over the years. He therefore went on to marry another woman outside the community. This was three years ago, and life has never been the same for Mrs Lukani and her four children. Sadly, and to complicate matters, when Chikondi, her last born daughter was born, she was found HIV-positive too.

Since then Mrs Lukani has moved on to accept the situation and head the family, to ensure that the children receive enough care. She spends most of the day looking for food and other basic needs to sustain the home. She says she has a

---

small scale business – selling doughnuts, although this does not consistently raise enough money to satisfy the family's basic needs. She further explains that she has a small garden in which she grows some maize. However, with her ailing health, she does not work regularly in her garden; the resulting poor yield does not last her for the whole year. This means she has to buy some food in the lean months (October to March) every year. She says it is very hard for her to look after the family with two of her children (Chikondi and her third born brother) HIV-positive.

Mrs Lukani adds that many women in the community face similar challenges resulting from disclosure of their HIV status to their husbands. She reiterates that while many women in the community are willing to go for VCT, most men refuse to do the same. Consequently, there are many divorces in the community. Mrs Lukani says she has accepted her situation and looks forward to the future although one of her greatest worries is the growth and development of her children whom she cherishes and who bring her consolation.

The issues raised in the case study

The key issues raised in the case study were reported by participants in the community, while some of the related information comes from recent research on childhood development and preschooling in Malawi.

(a) Poverty and general lack of food

From the story of the Lukani family, it is evident that poverty is a critical and often the main problem faced by families and children in rural areas. Various related studies and literature have clearly shown that most families in rural areas of Malawi and other parts of Africa cannot afford three meals per day; one meal per day is the most common scenario in most rural areas (Fisher *et al*, 2009; Kholowa, 2007; Swadener *et al*, 2000). This situation means that children do not receive optimum support in terms of their nutritional needs. Chikondi Lukani in our case study is in a typical scenario, which eventually threatens her future development.

(b) Difficulties in income generation for the family

In most cases families in Malawi do not have the support they need to empower them with skills and financial bases for their social-economic advancement, consequently, families fail to support themselves. This is evident in our case study family, whose situation is aggravated by their HIV status. This makes it all the more important that enough good food is available.

(c) Socio-cultural challenges

Our case study raises a number of issues with regard to social and cultural issues concerning childhood in Malawi. The HIV pandemic has brought about social imbalance in the community through disintegration of the family unit. In addition, the issue of expectations in terms of the roles of men and women in society is very important here: in fact this effectively raises the issue of social responsibility for children after the disintegration of the family at community level. For instance, one wonders whether it should be the responsibility of the woman to look after children; rather it should be a shared responsibility between husband and wife. It is critical that Malawi should put into place legal structures to ensure that children's rights and security are respected in times of such challenges.

(d) Weak social structures in support of the family and childhood in general

Literature shows that within the traditional extended family system in Africa, there are collective mechanisms for preparing and supporting children's physical, emotional, social and intellectual development through traditional games, stories, toys, songs, and ways of playing that are passed on from the older to the younger children (Evans, 1994). Thus despite the influence of westernisation, urbanisation and formal education, Africans have retained a reservoir of knowledge, practices and values for child development (Nsamenang, 2008; Prochner and Kabiru, 2008).

While such structures may exist in Chikondi's context, they are weakened by the high poverty levels, which eventually push the individuals and families towards individualism. The extended family system in Malawi and Africa continues to be threatened by globalisation and economic challenges, forcing many communities to move slowly towards individual rather than communal orientation to living and therefore care of children (Swadener *et al*, 2000). This has aggravated many children's already poor development opportunities, especially in rural settings. The CBCC is one of the key social structures at community level that may provide critical psycho-social care to complement any childcare service at home and in the community. However, the CBCC has its own challenges: inadequate food, play materials, teaching and learning resources, unqualified caregivers and poor infrastructure, all of which have implications for the quality of care and education provided to the children in the respective communities.

The CBCC in Chikondi's community is in such a situation though children are fed at least one meal a day and have the opportunity to play with the few locally made play structures at the CBCC. Despite these provisions, Chikondi faces other challenges at the CBCC as a consequence of her HIV status. For instance, she fails to concentrate in class because of the stigma. We were told that the other children come to know those who are infected, based on leaked information about their status within the community. Consequently, Chikondi, together with six other children in a similar situation at the CBCC are often mocked by fellow children about their status, and at one point some children did not want to associate with Chikondi until the caregivers at the CBCC intervened. Worse still, some of the parents who send their children to the CBCC protested about their children associating with HIV-positive children. However, the CBCC staff called a community meeting to educate the parents and guardians on the spread of HIV and AIDS and dispel their fears.

Thus, much as the CBCC may be considered beneficial to the children and the community as a whole, many questions can be raised about the extent to which the environment within the CBCC is helpful to children living in difficult circumstances. Kabiru and Njenga (2007) point out the need for special support, care and protection for children living under appalling situations to assist them cope and develop better, whether in the home or at a centre. Special needs in care centres (especially CBCCs) are sensitively handled, but have so far received limited attention in Malawi. Partly this is due to the huge lack of professional staff or caregivers and basic resources in ECD centres. It is therefore critical that while the nation focuses on issues of access to ECD services, special attention should also be given to this aspect to ensure that such children are not left out.

(e) Community involvement in the promotion of childhood

Recent research in Malawi has shown that most communities appreciate the benefits of CBCCs to children, parents and the community as a whole. For instance, the child is well prepared for primary school; parents are able to do other work at home while children are at CBCC. Community development is also facilitated through infrastructure improvement and the attraction of other related services for children (Fisher *et al*, 2009; Chibwana, 2007).

Consequently, many parents are willing to contribute material resources to sustain the CBCC. However, community involvement is only limited to mobilisation of material resources rather than helping with some of the core learning activities at the CBCC (Kholowa, 2007). This has implications for children's development. Chikondi has limited opportunity for optimum development both in the home and CBCC, presenting her with many dilemmas and insecurity not only for her future, but also her contribution to the socio-economic development of her family, the rural community and

Malawi as a whole. This consequence is highlighted when we further consider the actual learning opportunities in terms of literacy and numeracy development at the CBCC.

(f) Home versus school literacy and numeracy development for Chikondi

Literacy is critical for determining personal growth, quality of life, self-image and the ability to function in the world, at national or societal level, and is therefore central to the smooth functioning and economic prosperity of a society through the development of a well educated, flexible and highly skilled workforce (McGaw *et al*, 1989 cited in Browne, 1999). In an oral society such as Malawi, there is potential for oral activities within the community including the home, to facilitate literacy development in children. However, the assumption is often made that people without a tradition of literacy are therefore without the 'typically literate capacity' (Finnegan, 1988).

In the light of the many challenges families face in the rural areas, there is likely to be less deliberate attempt to facilitate children's literacy and numeracy potential in the home despite the indigenous resources available in the rural communities, such as folk tales, songs, puns, among others (Phiri, 2004). This is worsened by the fact that the majority of the homes cannot afford to buy books or related print materials to help children develop their literacy skills. Although currently there is no research into home literacy and numeracy practices in Malawi to use as evidence, we argue that at home, parents and guardians are likely to be more worried about and focus their attention on sustaining the home than children's literacy and numeracy development. Therefore most children from rural families are likely to be less prepared for centre based learning. Research evidence on provision of learning experiences, especially early literacy and numeracy in rural preschools, shows that such experiences are provided accidentally as most caregivers do not deliberately plan for literacy development activities and, worse still, caregivers do not even know they are providing early literacy experiences (Kholowa, 2007). In those preschools where caregivers make attempts to provide these, there is little exploitation of many of the activities that could help children to make strides in early literacy or numeracy development.

Note by editors: An announcement in *Prism* (244 October 2009:9) states that: 'Academics in Africa and at Strathclyde University are joining forces to transform literacy teaching in primary schools in Malawi by pioneering an official network of literacy educators'. Sue Ellis, co-author of this Chapter, stresses in that announcement that teaching children to read and write in Malawi presents particular challenges, for the reasons outlined in this Chapter.

Conclusion

Families and children in rural areas of Malawi face a myriad of challenges, which eventually have a great impact on children's growth and development. These range from huge lack of basic needs in the home especially food, clothes, water, etc and poor social facilities for children. HIV and AIDS have worsened the predicament for families and children. There is therefore a great need for policy and implementation strategies to be more realistic in addressing childhood needs, especially in the rural areas. Government and other stakeholders' urgent and strong commitment is needed now more than ever to rescue many children from the cycle of poverty and limited future participation in the social and economic development of Malawi.

Points for discussion

- What problems face young children in rural areas in Malawi in addition to those encountered by children in rural areas with which you are familiar?

- How might early education be made more accessible to such children?

References

Browne, A (1999) *Teaching Writing at Key Stage 1 and Before*. London: Paul Chapman

Chalamanda, F R W (2004) Co-coordinating the Development and Implementation of Malawi's National Plan of Action (NPA) for survival, protection and development of children. Unpublished Bachelor's project report, University of Victoria, Victoria, British Columbia, Canada

Chibwana, K (2007) Community based childcare centres (CBCC) resource assessment: the case of Zomba, Unpublished MA dissertation, University of Victoria, Canada

Evans, J L (1994) Childrearing practices in Africa: an introduction to the studies. In *Coordinator's Notebook, No.15* www.ecdgroup.com/download/cc115bca.pdf) Accessed May 2009

Finnegan, R H (1988) *Literacy and Orality: studies in the technology of communication*. Oxford: Basil Blackwell

Fisher, W, Kholowa, F, Chibwana, K and Silo, L (2009) *Positive Deviance Study of Community Based Childcare Centres* (CBCCs) in Malawi. Lilongwe: UNICEF

Government of Malawi (GoM) (2002) *Malawi Poverty Reduction Strategy Paper*. Lilongwe: Ministry of Finance and Planning

Kabiru, M and Njenga, A (2007) *Child Development*. Nairobi: FOCUS Publications

Kholowa, F A C (2007) Early literacy development opportunities for rural pre-school children in Malawi: case study of four pre-schools in Zomba District. Unpublished PhD thesis, University of Malawi/Sussex

Ministry of Gender and Community Services (MoGCS) (2003) *National Policy on Orphans and Vulnerable Children*. Lilongwe: MoGCS

MoWCD-UNICEF (2006) *Community Based Child Care Centres (CBCCs): past, present, and future: a study of community based child care centres in Malawi*. Lilongwe: UNICEF

Munthali, A, Mvula, P and Silo, L (2007). *Inventory for Community Based Child Care Centres (CBCC) (Report from the first eight districts).* Lilongwe: UNICEF

National AIDS Commission (NAC) (2003) HIV/AIDS in *Malawi: Estimates of the Prevalence of Infection and the Implications.* Zomba: Malawi National Statistics Office

National Statistics Office (NSO) (2002) 2002 *Malawi Core Welfare Indicators Questionnaire Survey: Report of Survey Results.* Zomba: Malawi National Statistics Office

National Statistical Office (NSO) (2003) *Malawi DHS EdData Survey 2002: Education Data for Decision-making.* Zomba: Malawi National Statistics Office

Nsamenang, A B (2008) (Mis)Understanding ECD in Africa: the force of local and global motives. In Garcia, M Pence, A and Evans, J (eds) (2008) *Africa's Future, Africa's Challenge: early childhood care and development in Sub-Saharan Africa.* Washington DC: The World Bank

Pence, A R (2004) *ECD Policy Development and Implementation in Africa* (Monograph), Early Childhood and Family Policy Series No. 9- 2004. Paris: UNESCO

Phiri, M (2004) Using Indigenous Materials for ECCD Curriculum in Malawi. Unpublished Bachelor's project report, University of Victoria, Victoria, British Columbia, Canada

Prochner, L and Kabiru, M (2008) ECD in Africa: A historical perspective. In Garcia, M, Pence, A and Evans, J (eds) (2008) *Africa's Future, Africa's Challenge: early childhood care and development in Sub-Saharan Africa.* Washington DC: The World Bank

Swadener, B B, Kabiru, M and Njenga, A (2000) *Does the Village Still Raise the Child? A collaborative study of changing child-rearing and early education in Kenya.* New York: State University of New York Press

8

Childhood in the World of AIDS in South Africa

Mary James

Background to South Africa

Children in South Africa are well provided for in the Constitution, which pays particular attention to children's rights, and sets an ideal for an environment where every child may flourish. There are additional safeguards to their rights to care and protection over and above the rights they have in common with all citizens (South Africa Constitution Bill of Rights, 1996). However, the reality for the majority of children in South Africa does not reflect these ideals. There are eighteen million children in South Africa, 39 per cent of the total population, and 54 per cent of them live in poorly resourced and under serviced rural areas. Some two million children live in the shacks of informal settlements with no clean water or sanitation and half of these children live in overcrowded conditions, more than four to a room, contributing to the spread of diseases. Diseases such as diarrhoea, respiratory infection and malnutrition account for 30 per cent of deaths in children under 5-years of age. Approximately 21 per cent of all children are orphans, defined by UNICEF as children without a living biological mother or father. Most have experienced bereavement before they even start school, and more than 120,000 children live in a household headed by a child (Proudlock *et al*, 2008).

Children are regarded as vulnerable when they are separated from caregivers, are malnourished, abused, neglected, out of school, disabled, ill, required to do excessive work, or lack access to services. These plus other factors contribute to the vulnerability of young children in Southern Africa. These factors include high rates of unemployment among caregivers resulting in extreme poverty; migrant labour that means parents work away from where their children live, failure to access government support grants, and little interest and support by families for their children's education. Children in rural black African families are particularly vulnerable as they are still 'most at risk of infant death, low birth weight, stunted growth, poor adjustment to school, increased repetition and school drop-out' (South African Government, Department of Education Department of Education, 2001:12). However, the most significant factor in the lives of young children in South Africa is the HIV/AIDS pandemic.

The impact of AIDS on young children in South Africa

HIV/AIDS remains the leading cause of death of children under 5 years of age, primarily due to transmission of the virus from mother to child during pregnancy and birth (Proudlock *et al*, 2008). Ninety per cent of all new infections in South Africa occur in young women aged between 15 and 24 years, the child-bearing years. Almost 40 per cent of pregnant mothers and one in five of all adults are infected. There were around 280,000 children aged below 15 years of age living with HIV in South Africa in 2007 (www.avert.org). For each person living with HIV, there are also families, friends and wider communities affected by it. AIDS puts immense pressure on single parents, extended families and community structures. The government provides few social safety nets and, when there is some provision, it is often not accessed by the most marginalised families.

The compound effects of chronic illness in the family increases children's vulnerability. When parents are bedridden or have died, young children are often left without consistent responsive care, and may become neglected. Their own health is compromised through infection, inadequate nutrition and poor health care. Their growth is retarded so that there is an increased chance of developmental delay. If the breadwinner is no longer able to earn, and there are increased medical costs, the household capacity to provide for basic needs declines. Impoverished and in some cases without parents to educate and protect them, vulnerable children face increased risk of abuse and HIV infection. Some are forced into work and others are sexually exploited in return for care, shelter or food (Richter, 2008).

Once they are receiving antiretroviral drug treatment, people who are HIV positive are able to regain their health and lead normal lives. Sadly, few people in South Africa have access to the drugs, and in 2007 fewer than 30 per cent of people in need were receiving treatment (www.avert.org).

AIDS deaths account for almost half of all deaths in South Africa, and for almost three quarters of the deaths of people aged between 15 and 49. The average life expectancy in South Africa is now 54 years and over half of 15-year-olds are not expected to reach the age of 60. Poverty and the responsibilities of caring for parents and siblings is a burden for children and may result in them withdrawing from school, even while their parents are still living. The illness and death of their parents creates fear and trauma for the children. There is a loss of hope for the future that is worsened by the stigma attached to HIV/AIDS and to being an orphan (Richter *et al*, 2006).

Stigma is common. HIV is regarded in most countries as a disease of the poor. Although there is some correlation between extreme poverty and the incidence of HIV in South Africa, infection is prevalent across all sectors of society. AIDS related stigma is, to a large extent, attributed to the fact that AIDS infection is seen to be a consequence of promiscuity, drug addiction, and prostitution, behaviours that are already stigmatised. Children orphaned by AIDS are more likely to be rejected by extended family members than those orphaned by other causes. Children whose parents are presumed to have died of AIDS are often thought to be HIV positive themselves, and as a consequence are excluded from school and denied treatment when they are sick. Children affected by AIDS are frequently marginalised and quickly become the most vulnerable members of society (www.avert.org).

Children dealing with the loss or serious illness of a caregiver must assume roles not usual for children. Once forced to take on these adult roles, children often become adultified. Childhood 'adultification' can happen in even very young children, if they are required to assume an adult role in the changed family circumstances. Adultified children must deal with the stresses and strains of adult responsibilities and obligations and, as a result, they often develop internal resources and skills far beyond their age, at the expense of age appropriate development in other areas.

Burton (2005) refers to forms of *adultification*, suggesting that there are four different forms of adultification, and each form presents both risk and resilience factors to the development of young children. Children affected by AIDS move across a continuum of these categories in response to the needs and circumstances of the family.

1. Precocious knowledge is common in poor families living in over-crowded conditions. Children become aware of the stress of parents and try to relieve this and to comfort them. In this form of adultification children seldom assume adult roles, but rather observe be-

haviours and gather and store information not appropriate to their age. Exposure to precocious knowledge may result in children emulating adult behaviour.

2   The most common form of adultification is mentored adultification which occurs when children take on adult-like roles but there is still some instruction from their parents or adult caregiver. Parents do not relinquish their authority but rely on their children to assume responsibilities with very little supervision. Children have a sense of self worth and feel valued. They grow in confidence and learn useful skills.

3   Peerified adultification puts a child in a position of operating as a parent's equal, for a short period or more permanently. The child must act more like a spouse than a child, and becomes the confidante of the parent.

4   Parentification is the most extreme form of adultification. This occurs when the child must assume the role of parent, either to siblings or even to terminally ill parents. Parentification is common for the large numbers of children affected by HIV/AIDS who must head households. These children learn new life skills but must cope with a huge emotional load and the loss of childhood.

A case study of the impact of AIDS on a family

The case study illustrates many of the consequences for children living in a family infected and affected by HIV/AIDS. It is set in a rural village in Kwa Zulu Natal, South Africa, a province with extremely high incidence of infection. The community is dominated by women because many of the men are absent, seeking work in cities around South Africa. Community leaders estimate that fewer than a quarter of the remaining adults are employed, mostly as labourers on nearby farms, and almost half of families live below the poverty line.

The homes are scattered and accessed on gravel roads. Most of the houses are rondavels, (traditional Zulu wattle and daub round houses), and although many have been electrified in the last five years, water is still collected from communal taps or the river, and pit latrines are the norm. There is no public transport and the private minibus taxis are expensive and unreliable. There are no medical facilities in the village, but itinerant health workers provide some primary health care, and a mobile clinic visits once a month.

A case study

Angel was born at the family home in Kwa Daga. Her mother was employed nearby as a housekeeper and nanny, leaving home before dawn and arriving home at dusk. Angel's father was seldom at home, but visited at the end of each month from his job at the sugar mill situated some 80 kilometers away, bringing some money and a few treats.

The family home consisted of two rondavels. There were no immediate neighbours, but the house was quite close to the river where they collected water each day. They had no electricity, relying on a fire at the centre of the rondavel for cooking and heating, and candles for light in the evening. Life was secure and happy. Angel, and her younger sister Precious, spent many hours with their Gogo (grandmother), who fed and cared for them while their parents were away. After school they helped with the chores. Firewood had to be collected, and fresh water carried up from the river. As Angel reported: 'These jobs never seemed like work when we were with Gogo. She made it seem like fun – we sang and she told us stories while we were busy'.

When Angel was 11, Gogo became ill and died as a result of TB. Angel and Precious now had the responsibility of doing the chores by themselves, either before or after school. Despite being so young, Angel was expected to make the fire and cook the meal before their mother returned. 'I felt as though nobody remembered that I was just a child. I wanted to spend time with my friends, and play. I hated doing all the chores on my own – Precious wouldn't listen to me – and my mother was often angry, especially after my father got sick. Sometimes he didn't work and we had only a little money.'

By the age of 13, Angel had become rebellious. She often returned home late after school, having spent time with friends – and soon with a series of boyfriends. 'I didn't care if Precious did the work now. I felt special because I was popular.' Despite the regular talks at school on the dangers of HIV and AIDS, Angel was sexually active before she was 14. At 15 she was pregnant but, afraid of her mother's reaction, she kept this a secret for as long as possible. The 16-year-old father refused to accept responsibility. Her mother discovered the truth when Angel was seven months pregnant. She was sent away to stay with relations in the city, more than 200 kilometres away. She had not met them before, and they gave her little attention or support. She was alone when Samkelo, her son, was born at the nearby clinic. She sent a message to her mother but received no reply.

When Samkelo was five weeks old Angel was asked to leave. She moved into a shared rented room. She managed to find a job as the night cashier at a 24 hour store. Most nights, she worked with Samkelo tied on her back. Despite her best efforts, Angel was not able to manage on her own. Her mother, concerned about the stigma she would face, still refused to let her come home, but she was taken in by her aunt in the nearby town. Angel was able to leave Samkelo at home while she continued to work at the store.

'This was a difficult time. Aunty was poor and old. I only earned a very small amount. Samkelo was often sick. He didn't grow well. Mostly there wasn't enough food. I did all the chores at home and worked at night. I was always tired. I wanted to go back to school, but then we would have had no money.' Angel took Samkelo to the clinic regularly because he was often ill. The staff suggested that he should be tested for HIV/AIDS. Angel refused. She had already been abandoned by her family and could not face more rejection. She believed that her health indicated that Samkelo could not be HIV positive. His milestones were slightly delayed, and he was underweight, but Samkelo began to walk and talk. Angel was by now employed at a day care centre, and was able to take Samkelo with her. The staff encouraged and supported Angel and her parenting skills improved. Samkelo, however, regressed. He spent much of the day sleeping and was no longer able to walk. Angel agreed to have him tested.

Samkelo was HIV positive and began to receive antiretroviral treatment.

Samkelo quickly improved, and regained a normal weight and appeared healthy. It was at this time that Angel realised that she was pregnant again. Worried that this baby would also be HIV positive, she decided that she would be tested. The results confirmed what she suspected; she was HIV positive.

The support of her counsellor and the clinic support group gave Angel the strength to cope. She made the bold decision to disclose her status. 'I believed that if I was honest and faced it, I could beat the sickness.' She still did not disclose Samkelo's status. Her mother was not willing to accept her, so Angel continued to face rejection and isolation. Learning that her unborn baby could be protected from the virus, she joined the prevention of mother to child transmission programme. Mbali, her daughter, is a calm, healthy baby who has been tested twice to confirm that she has escaped infection.

Within weeks of Mbali's birth, Angel's family increased again. Precious, who had been unwell for some time, died and Angel took in her two-year-old son, Fano. She again had to face the ordeal of having a child tested, and the rigours of anti-retroviral treatment. The boys are healthy, happy little boys, but their childhood will never be what most people perceive as typical. Angel needs to prepare Samkelo and Fano to live safe and healthy lives. From a very early age, they have known the routine of taking medication daily, at the same time. They have had to learn to deal with their own cuts and bruises. Angel has chosen to teach them this without revealing their HIV status. 'They are only children – they won't understand that they should not talk about this.' When I question her more, she explains that she has learnt to deal with the stigma, but wants to protect the children. She wants them to be included in school activities, to be allowed to play with others and not to be called names. She never allows them to sleep over at friends, because she worries that the medicine may be forgotten, and that they will be stigmatised if people know the children are on antiretroviral treatment.

Mbali, ironically, also feels different from other children. She sometimes asks why she is not being cared for as she does not take medication and does not attend the clinic. She had also been rejected by their grandmother. Angel worries too about what would happen to her children if she became ill and could not look after them.

The stigma of AIDS

Aside from the numbers of deaths and the physical suffering, stigma is still perhaps the most serious issue connected to the AIDS pandemic.

Stigma remains the single most important barrier to public action. It is a main reason why too many people are afraid to see a doctor to determine whether they have the disease, or to seek treatment if so. Stigma is a chief reason why the AIDS epidemic continues to devastate societies around the world. (Ban Ki-Moon, 2006)

Possibly the greatest cause for stigma is fear. People fear the illness, and fear dying from it. There is still a great deal of myth and misinformation about the disease, including the belief that it is contagious through physical contact. This makes people afraid of mixing with those who live with HIV and AIDS, and even with their surviving family. HIVstigma is layered with other stigmas such as poverty, drug abuse and casual sex. People who have tested positive are judged and blamed for their behaviour, receiving little sympathy and help.

By contrast, the majority of aid programmes concentrate their efforts on *AIDS orphans.* In HIV affected communities, where extreme poverty and poor re-sourcing are prevalent, orphans are seldom worse off than other vulnerable children. The limited focus on orphans has meant that children living with sick parents may not receive help, and large numbers of vulnerable children and their families may be overlooked. Families, and the communities in which they live, are the best hope for supporting vulnerable children, and they require ongoing assistance from outside so that they can care for their children. It is crucial that aid responses take a long-term view and include children and their families as active participants in fighting HIV/AIDS and improving their own lives. Many relief programmes regard children as 'helpless victims', and concentrate their support on providing handouts of money, food and clothing. This tends to reinforce dependency, and can exacerbate the stigma and discrimination against them.

Adultified children face their own stigma. These children have had to take charge in their families; they make important long term decisions regarding finances and siblings. They have become adults in children's bodies. As a result many resent authority, and develop a tendency to worry excessively. This may result in problems at school, and with the extended family where they are labelled as precocious and undisciplined. However, not all the effects of adultification are negative. Many of these children develop great leadership qualities. Adultified children are often more self reliant, responsible and demonstrate greater resilience than other children. Angel's experiences show this.

Conclusions

Internationally, there are many agencies working to mitigate the effects of the HIV/AIDS pandemic on children. The most successful responses consider families and communities as the foundation for change, and children are included in the process. Key strategies of the internationally recognised framework for the protection, care and support of orphans and vulnerable children living in a world with HIV/AIDS are:

1. strengthen the capacity of families to protect and care for orphans and vulnerable children by prolonging the lives of parents and providing economic, psychosocial and other support
2. mobilise and support community-based responses
3. ensure access for orphans and vulnerable children to essential services, including education, health care, birth registration and others
4. ensure that governments protect the most vulnerable children through improved policy and legislation and by channelling resources to families and communities
5. raise awareness at all levels through advocacy and social mobilisation to create a supportive environment for children and families affected by HIV/AIDS.

See for example A framework for the protection, care and support of orphans and vulnerable children living in a world with HIV/AIDS www.ovcsupport. net/graphics/OVC/documents/0000292e.pdf

Points for discussion

■ Make a note of the information on HIV/AIDS that you have learnt from this Chapter and consider how much of it is relevant beyond South Africa.

■ What could be done to remove the stigma attached to HIV/AIDS?

■ Consider the pros and cons of different degrees of adultification as referred to in this Chapter.

References

Ban, Ki-Moon (2006) The stigma factor. Biggest hurdle to combat HIV/AIDS. *Washington Times.* August www.washingtontimes.com/news/2008/aug/06/the-stigma-factor Accessed August 2009

Burton, L (2005) Improving linkages between research, practice and policy. Session 428 October 2005. Paper at The Salzburg Seminar. Improving linkages between research, practice and policy.

Proudlock, P, Dutschke, M, Jamieson, L, Monson, J and Smith C (eds) (2008) *South African Child Gauge 2007/2008.* Cape Town: Children's Institute, University of Cape Town

Richter, L (2008) *No Small Issue: children and families.* Universal Action Now. Plenary Presentation at the XVII International AIDS Conference Universal Action Now, Mexico City, Mexico, 6 August 2008. *Online Outreach Paper 3.* The Hague, The Netherlands: Bernard van Leer Foundation

Richter, L, Foster, G and Sherr, L (2006) *Where the Heart is: meeting the psychosocial needs of young children in the context of HIV/AIDS.* The Hague, The Netherlands: Bernard van Leer Foundation (obtainable on www.hsrc.ac.za Accessed August 2009

South African Government Constitution, Bill of Rights (1996) www.info.gov.za/documents/constitution/1996/96cons2.htm#28 Accessed August 2009

South African Government Department of Education (2001) *Education White Paper 5 on Early Childhood Development.* Pretoria: Government Printers

Websites

Convention on the Rights of the Child. (1989) http://ohchr.org/english/law/crc.htm Accessed August 2009

Medical Research Council http://www. mrc.ac.za Accessed August 2009

UNICEF (2006) South Africa: Statistics http://www.unicef.org/infobycountry/southafrica_statistics.html Accessed March 2008

For information on AIDS/HIV www.avert.org/aidsstigma.htm Accessed August 2009

Section III
Changing Generations

It is nothing new for major changes to occur from one generation to the next; most grandparents see the world in a very different light from their grandchildren. There are claims that such changes have accelerated over the past hundred years. The three Chapters in this section highlight the traumas faced by young children and their families in troubled times. In Chapter 9, two generations growing up in an urban area in war torn Northern Ireland are contrasted. Chapter 10 is set in Romania, where families have recently faced major changes in the political philosophy of those ruling the country, with consequences for the care and education of young children. Chapter 11, set in urban USA, describes the lives of a family of refugees for whom everything has changed as they moved, from rural to urban life and to a different culture, yet where the resilience of the family has led to successful integration.

- When you read each of these Chapters consider not only the problems faced by the young children but also those faced by their parents and their teachers.
- As you read, make a note of further information you need in order to understand more fully these young children's experiences of early education.

9

War and Peace in Northern Ireland: childhood in transition

Glenda Walsh and Dorothy McMillan

Introduction

> The true measure of a nation's standing is how well it attends to its children – their health and safety, their material security, their education and socialisation, and their sense of being loved, valued and included in the families and societies into which they are born. (UNICEF, 2007:1)

But for some nations, none more so than Northern Ireland, the reality of childhood for many of its children has been entirely different and has fallen far short of the above expectations. Quoting the words of the Irish singer Paul Brady, Ruddy (1996:96) suggests that, 'Up here' in Northern Ireland 'we sacrifice our children, to feed the worn out dreams of yesterday'.

Northern Ireland, the smallest of the four devolved nations within the United Kingdom, with a population of approximately 1.5 million, is world renowned for its natural beauty, such as the Glens of Antrim, the Giant's Causeway, Enniskillen Lakes and the Mountains of Mourne that sweep down to the sea. However, against this picturesque landscape, in forty different shades of green, Northern Ireland is infamous for its beleaguered, troubled past, when for nearly a quarter of a century, from the late 1960s to the mid 1990s, it has been fraught with political and sectarian violence, described by Borooah (1995:133) as a 'theatre of war'.

Such conflict, euphemistically known as *The Troubles*, finds its origins in the Ulster Plantation, when Protestants from England and Scotland were introduced into Ireland by the English monarchy and tensions between Catholics and Protestants arose almost immediately. This unrest culminated in the Anglo-Irish war of 1919-1921, which resulted in the partitioning of Ireland into two States, the Irish Free State and Northern Ireland which was ruled by its own Parliament in Belfast, known as Stormont, until 1972. From its inception, Northern Ireland contained a large minority of Catholics who opposed partition and were unsympathetic to the new state's existence.

Sectarianism erupted into violence in the 1920s and 1930s and such unrest came to the fore in the late 1960s with the Civil Rights movement until in August 1969, the Troubles we know of today began. Despite the imposition of direct rule from 1972, unremitting violence continued and peace was not restored to Northern Ireland until the paramilitary ceasefires in 1994 (see Walsh, 2007). Such conflict has resulted in over 3,600 deaths and well over 40,000 people being injured (Morrissey and Smyth, 2002). Furthermore, high levels of residential, social and educational segregation have arisen, so that, according to Kelly and Sinclair (2003), 95 per cent of children attend religiously segregated schools and 80 per cent of housing is also segregated according to religion.

Children and young people have also suffered greatly. According to Save the Children (2005) 391 children under the age of 18 and 875 young people aged 18-24 were killed in the violence in Northern Ireland. Not only did some children lose their lives, but many experienced emotional and psychological effects (Ewart and Schubotz, 2004) through the loss of family members, witnessing violence and murders and the experiences of rioting and bombs. Drawing on a number of research studies, the Belfast Interface Project (1997) reports that just under 20 per cent of 10- and 11-year-olds growing up in Northern Ireland at that time had either been in, or been close to, a bomb explosion. The same percentage had a friend or relative killed or injured in the troubles and 90 per cent of 9- to 11-year-olds had seen a hijacked vehicle burning, 50 per cent had seen gun shootings, and 37 per cent had witnessed bomb explosions. On a more universal level Ewart and Schubotz (2004) argue that most, if not all, children and young people have to some extent been influenced by the Troubles in some shape or form, particularly in the formation of their attitudes and the construction of religious and societal divides, oppression and discrimination.

The children perhaps most affected by the Troubles are those who live in the interface areas of inner city Belfast. These areas are zones of tension and violence, situated largely within the realm of public housing and are characterised by marginalisation, poverty, social exclusion and limited access to resources (Jarman, 2005). O'Reilly and Browne (2001) indicate that people who live in these poorer households, and particularly children, tend to have borne the brunt of the Troubles much more than those from wealthier homes. However, the question remains as to whether the nightmare for Northern Ireland citizens, especially children, has finally come to an end with the restoration of peace, resulting from the 1994 ceasefires and the Belfast Agreement of 1998. This Chapter will present the childhood experiences of Frances and Billy, both of whom were born in interface areas of inner city Belfast, Frances during the Troubles and Billy during the peace process. Each story will highlight how the economical, educational and political issues at that time have impacted on each of Frances' and Billy's childhoods. The Chapter will conclude with a synopsis of how childhood has changed during times of conflict and peace in Northern Ireland and a picture of what the future may hold.

Frances' story

Frances was born on 21 October 1972 into a family of seven. She lived with her mother (Bridget), her father (Sean) and four other siblings, Eoghan (7), Liam (5), Siobhan (3) and Mary (2) in a housing estate off the Falls Road, an interface area in West Belfast. Her family was republican and her father was a member of the Irish Republican Army (IRA). Both of her parents were unemployed. Her mother had become pregnant at the age of 16, immediately after leaving school, and despite her father's efforts to gain employment as a labourer, all were in vain and he suffered from depression as a result.

Such a situation is not unique to Frances' family as, according to Borooah (1995), Catholics were discriminated against particularly in two domains, access to public sector jobs and housing.

Extreme poverty was experienced by Frances' family. Quality food and clothing were limited, holidays were non-existent, toys were few and they did not have a garden to play in. Local play parks and other outdoor facilities were few in number and those that did exist tended to be badly vandalised, causing children to play amongst inappropriate debris and in unsafe surroundings. Although Frances and her siblings were eligible for a free lunch every day at primary school, rarely was a substantial, healthy meal served on the dinner table in Frances' home; vegetables and meat were a novelty. Frances recounts how she got excited when she would be invited to stay over at her cousin's house as she got orange juice to drink there, instead of water.

Childhood poverty was and still is a real issue in conflict areas such as West Belfast (see Horgan, 2005). Despite some form of family support in terms of unemployment and child benefits, which tends to be similar to that in the United Kingdom, Horgan (2005) argues that child poverty is exacerbated by the high cost of living in Northern Ireland as compared to other parts of the UK and Ireland, impacting on children's emotional and physical well being.

Frances' educational experience began in September 1977, when she entered Year 1 in her local maintained primary school (ie for Catholic children only). Preschool places were limited during the1970s, when a total of 58 nursery schools and 41 nursery units were established (McMillan, 2008). Although in 1965 the Northern Ireland regional branch of the Preschool Playgroups Association (PPA) was formed as (NIPPA) and made rapid progress, McMillan (2008) explains that much of the growth had taken place in middle class areas and that there was a need for development in poorer areas of Belfast.

As a consequence of having no preschool experience and having been cared for by her mother, Frances' entry into Year 1 was her first experience of leaving the home environment. The school Frances attended was very traditional both in ethos and curriculum, a description applied to most schools throughout NI at that time (see Caul, 1990), and little effort was made on the school's part to ease the transition for young children like Frances from home to school. Frances recalls how she was expected on the first day to leave her mother at the front door and to sit at a table, beside peers whom she had never met, and complete written literacy and numeracy worksheets. Little emphasis was placed on play and child-initiated learning. An authoritarian pedagogy pervaded the entire school system. Such a disciplined approach increased as Frances progressed through primary school, corporal punishment still in existence.

No formal primary curriculum was in place during Frances' education, but literacy and numeracy were prioritised as the 11+, the process of selection at the end of primary school, determined what was taught in the classroom (see Walsh, 2007). Reflecting on her educational experience in the home, Frances explains that little pressure was put on her by her parents to complete her homework or engage in further educational experiences. Her parents had failed at every stage of the education system and therefore placed no value on their children succeeding in it. Expectations on the teachers' part for children like Frances were also low and it was only those children whom the teachers felt would succeed in the selection process who would be offered the opportunity and preparation to do so. Aspirations regarding higher or further education for Frances and her siblings were non-existent. Such a pattern of behaviour is quite common place in the most troubled and socially deprived areas of Belfast (Muldoon *et al*, 2000).

The Troubles were rife during Frances' childhood and no more so than in West Belfast. Frances and her family frequently had to evacuate their home and shootings and bombings were a regular occurrence. Children were not exempt from such violence and destruction. Having been playing outside close to an army barracks, Frances recounts how, at the age of 7, she was first on the scene of a mutilated body caused by an explosion. Frances explains how she at first felt a sense of thrill and excitement, but that such an image has been imprinted on her mind for life. Writers such as Ruddy (1996) and Steele-Perkins (2008) indicate how this was not a one off occurrence but that many children, particularly in these interface areas, had similar gruesome experiences.

Sectarianism was also rampant. Frances and her siblings were often on the receiving end of name calling and physical aggression as they walked home from school, due to the uniform they wore or the sports equipment they carried. Similarly, in the home, Frances' father would constantly remind his children of their republican roots and how they should be willing to 'fight for the cause'. A hatred of the Royal Ulster Constabulary (the police service at that time) was instilled into the children and anything that was associated with Great Britain such as the British flag, the British army and even the Royal Family.

When reflecting on her childhood, Frances describes it as 'grim', 'bleak' and 'dismal'. For her, childhood was an existence, ie surviving each day, rather than looking forward to the future. In one way she explains how she was expected to grow up too quickly; whilst in another way she often yearned for a form of escapism for a better life, where she often cried out for help, but little help seemed available (Ruddy, 1996: Horgan, 2005). But, now that help has arrived in the Peace Process, has childhood improved for children living in interface areas? The next case study will help to shine some light on this issue.

Billy's story

Billy was born on 3 June 2002 into a family of five: his mother Lizzie, his father William and two older sisters Julie (5) and Vicky (3). They live in West Belfast in a housing estate in the Shankill Road area. Lizzie stays at home to look after the children, while her husband works in a local factory as a window fitter. Both of Billy's parents have lived on the Shankill Road all their lives. William left school at 16 with five GCSEs and, having left school with three GCSEs, Lizzie worked as a cleaner in the City Hospital but had to give up when she started a family, due to the cost of child care. Lizzie had her first child at the age of 18 and she and William (20 years old) were married the following year.

Although financially times are difficult, with only one parent in full time employment, Billy's economic circumstances are much superior to those of Frances. Family support has improved greatly since the 1970s. William is eligible for both Working and Child Tax Credits which supplement his income and Child Benefit and Maternity Allowance have increased also (see Walsh, 2007). Unlike Frances' family, Billy's parents own their own house and car and they usually have a holiday each year. They live in a terraced house which has three bedrooms and one bathroom upstairs with an additional toilet downstairs. It has a small patch of garden both at the front and at the rear. Although Billy and his siblings are not eligible for free school meals, Lizzie tries to ensure that the children eat a well-balanced diet but as people tend to make dietary choices based on their finances, this does not always result in a highly nutritional diet.

Despite Billy's lifestyle appearing much superior to that of Frances, child poverty, particularly in West Belfast and in other conflict areas across Northern Ireland, is still extremely high. Monteith and McLaughlin (2006) indicate that between one quarter and one third of children living in Northern Ireland are growing up in poverty, resulting in poor dental care, malnutrition, high levels of asthma and increasing levels of child obesity. Particularly since the turn of the millennium, children's health and wellbeing have been elevated on the political agenda, culminating in the publication of the Ten Year Strategy (OFMDFM, 2006). This policy document stresses that each child and young person should be:

> healthy, enjoying, learning and achieving, living in safety and with stability, experiencing economic and environmental wellbeing, contributing positively to the community and society and living in a society which respects their rights. (OFMDFM, 2006:7)

Earlier the Northern Ireland Office of Commissioner for Children and Young People (NICCY) was created to promote and protect the rights and best interests of children and young people in Northern Ireland and a strategy focusing specifically on Early Years is due for publication in 2009. With these measures in place, the future in terms of health and wellbeing for Billy and his siblings certainly looks more hopeful.

Educationally the picture for Billy also appears more promising as children and family services have expanded rapidly over the past ten years (Walsh,

2007). Having attended a weekly parent and toddler group with his mother, Billy began a local playgroup at the age of 3 and then, in his preschool year, he attended a local nursery unit, attached to the primary school where he would go the subsequent year. Both the playgroup and the nursery follow the Pre-school Curricular Guidance (DHSS, CCEA and DENI, 1997, revised in 2006), which emphasises the importance of young children's holistic development through the medium of play. The transition from preschool to primary school was less traumatic for Billy than for Frances, as he attended a primary school which was piloting the Early Years Enriched Curriculum (see Walsh *et al*, 2006).

Since the Education Reform Order, Northern Ireland (Great Britain, 1989) Northern Ireland children have been obliged to commence primary school in the September after their fourth birthday and to follow the demands of a curriculum that was subject-based and assessment led. Since 1999, however CCEA have been revising the primary curriculum and one of their priorities is to make the early years of primary schooling more developmentally appropriate and play-based in perspective. The pilot of this intervention was known as the Enriched Curriculum and from 2008 it has been rolled out across all Year 1 and 2 classes in Northern Ireland. (For more detailed information see Sproule *et al*, 2005 and Walsh *et al*, 2006). As Walsh (2007:68) argues, 'such a development paves the way for an exciting but challenging future for Early Years education in general'.

This pedagogical approach in the Early Years particularly suits Billy as he entered Year 1 at only 4 years and 2 months and, instead of being switched off learning at an early age, Billy developed a positive disposition towards learning. He is now about to enter Year 4, and, although not the brightest in the class, he enjoys school and tries hard and his academic future looks quite positive. His parents both encourage him and his siblings to do their homework and have high aspirations for their children's future. However at times they appear to put too much pressure on their children to achieve where they failed, advocating the use of computer games rather than outdoor play, parental behaviour that appears to have become almost endemic throughout the United Kingdom (Clark, 2007 and Sylvester and Thompson, 2007).

Politically the situation, at least in rhetoric, appears more positive for Billy. Billy was born in a time of so-called peace and stability in Northern Ireland when the ceasefires had taken placed and the Belfast Agreement was in place, described by Donnelly *et al* (2006:1) as a 'historic milestone' in Northern Ireland, providing a strategy to resolve the conflict of the past thirty years.

Positive initiatives have been detailed in the Ten Year Strategy (OFMDFM, 2006) as to the creation of a much more inclusive society and monies have been invested by outside agencies in early years programmes such as the Media Initiative (Connolly *et al*, 2006) and Sesame Tree (Walsh and Kehoe, 2007) to encourage children to respect differences and become more tolerant of others from an early age. It would seem that Billy and his siblings will be subjected to less violence and psychological anxiety and to some extent this is the case, as Donnelly *et al* (2006) indicate that political violence is currently at a much lower level than that of the 1970s and 1980s.

However, this does not suggest that conflict and sectarianism have been totally eradicated. Drawing on their research with children from interface areas across Northern Ireland, McAlister *et al* (2009) suggest that echoes of the past are reverberating today. According to the children interviewed, a virus of sectarianism still penetrates these interface areas, where there is a lack of trust in the police service, a resentment towards the politicians and violence is still part of everyday life, due to emerging problems such as drink and drugs. Donnelly *et al* (2006) support these findings, indicating that, since the Belfast Agreement, relationships between the two communities may actually have become more polarised, rather than united. Despite Billy only being 7-years-old, he knows that he is a Protestant and he describes himself as a 'Prod' and calls the Catholics who live on the other side of the peace wall 'Wee Fenians'.

Although his father does not align himself with any paramilitary organisation, he sees himself as a loyalist but is in favour of peace and does not want a return to the past. Billy's grandfather, however, was a member of the Ulster Volunteer Force and tries to ensure that his children and grandchildren do not forget the actions of their forefathers, and reminds them of the deeds of the IRA in an effort to keep past loyalties alive. As Ewart and Schubotz (2004:15) suggest, 'the attitudes of family members are perhaps the most influential factor in shaping children's and young people's attitudes to sectarianism'.

Conclusion

The transition in childhood from a time of war to a time of peace in Northern Ireland has essentially been positive. Billy appears to be experiencing a healthier and more comfortable lifestyle and he has enjoyed a more positive and beneficial start to his education than that available to Frances. However, despite many initiatives being put in place to help children and young people look forward to a shared future, Walsh (2007) argues that many of these pledges appear philanthropic but not realistic as changing mindsets will not take place overnight in a society slowly emerging from conflict. The future in this domain certainly does not augur well with the onset of a deep financial recession, which is already resulting in the loss of jobs. Furthermore, in addition to deep-rooted sectarianism, racism is becoming rife in Northern Ireland, particularly in these deprived areas (Donnelly *et al*, 2006), and drug related violence is also increasing rapidly. As Mr Olara Otunna, the Special Representative of the Secretary General of the United Nations on Children and Armed Conflict, states:

> Following conflict, the prospects of recovery often depend largely on giving priority attention to young people in the rebuilding process, rehabilitating young people affected by war, and restoring their sense of hope. ... All key actors responsible ... should make the rights and protection of children a central concern in their planning, programming and resource allocation. (cited in Horgan, 2005 unpaginated)

It would seem that Northern Ireland has started a journey to improving childhood in the twenty-first century but it has still a long way to go.

Points for discussion

■ Reflecting on the two case studies, can you identify any improvements in Billy's childhood as compared to that of Frances? If so, what, in your opinion, caused these improvements?

■ Both Frances and Billy come from socially deprived areas in Northern Ireland. Choose a socially deprived area in the community where you live and consider the impact poverty is having on young children's childhood.

References

Belfast Interface Project (1997) *Work with Young People in Interface Areas*. Belfast: Belfast Interface Project

Borooah, V K (1995) Symposium on the Economic Implications of Peace in Ireland, *Journal of the Statistical and Social Inquiry Society of Ireland*. XXVII (Part II) p133-144

Caul, L (ed) (1990) *Schools under Scrutiny: the case of NI*. London: MacMillan Education

Clark, L (2007) Over-protective parents robbing children of their childhood, experts warn. *Daily Mail*, 10 September 2007

Connolly, P, Fitzpatrick, S, Gallagher, T and Harris, P (2006) Addressing a diversity and inclusion in the Early Years in conflict-affected societies: a case study of the media initiative for children – Northern Ireland. *International Journal of Early Years Education*. 14(3) p263-278

DHSS, CCEA and DENI, (1997, 2006) *Curricular Guidance for Pre-school Education*. Belfast: CCEA

Donnelly, C, Osborne, B and McKeown, P (2006) Introduction: pluralism, devolution and education in Northern Ireland. In Donnelly, C, Osborne, B and McKeown, P (eds) *Devolution and Pluralism in Education in Northern Ireland*, Manchester: Manchester University Press

Ewart, S and Schubotz, D (2004) *Voices behind the Statistics: young children's views of sectarianism in Northern Ireland*. London: NCB

Great Britain (1989) *Education Reform (Northern Ireland) Order*. Belfast: HMSO

Horgan, G (2005) The particular circumstances of children in Northern Ireland. Available at http://www.childrenslawcentre.org/ParticularCircumstancesofChildreninNorthernIreland-Goretti Horgan.htm Accessed June 2009

Jarman, N (2005) Changing places, moving boundaries: the development of new interface areas. Available at http://www.community-relations.org.uk/filestore/documents/shared-space-issue-1-b-neil-jarman.pdf Accessed June 2009

Kelly, B and Sinclair, R (2003) *Children from Cross Community Families in Public Care in Northern Ireland*. London: National Children's Bureau (NCB)

McAlister, S (2009) Childhood in transition: the rights of children and young people in high conflict communities. Paper presented at the conference entitled 'The UNCRC at 20 – A Multidisciplinary Approach' on 7 May 2009 at Queen's University, Belfast

McMillan, D (2008) Education and Care: Implications for Educare Training in Northern Ireland, Unpublished PhD thesis, Belfast: Queen's University Belfast

Monteith, E and McLaughlin, M (2006) *Child and Family Poverty*. Belfast: OFMDFM

Morrissey, M and Smyth, M (2002) *Northern Ireland after the Good Friday Agreement*. London: Pluto Press

Muldoon, O, Trew, K and Kilpatrick, R (2000) The legacy of the troubles on the young people's psychological and social development and their school life. *Youth and Society* 32(1) p6-28

O'Reilly D and Browne S (2001) *Health and Health Service Use in Northern Ireland: social variations*. Belfast: Department of Health, Social Services and Public Safety

Office for the Minister and Deputy First Minister – OFMDFM (2006) *Our Children and Young People – Our Pledge*. Belfast: OFMDFM

Ruddy, B (1996) Children in Northern Ireland – a lost generation. *International Journal of Early Childhood Education*, 28(1) p67-72

Save the Children (2005) Key themes for Save the Children in Northern Ireland. Available at www.savethechildren.org.uk Accessed May 2009

Sproule, L, McGuiness, C, Trew, K, Rafferty, H, Walsh, G, Sheehy, N and O'Neill, B (2005) *The Early Years Enriched Curriculum Evaluation Project: Final Report Phase 1* (end of fourth year). Belfast: CCEA

Steele-Perkins, C (2008) War and Peace: life in Belfast after the troubles. Available at http://women.timesonline.co.uk/tol/life_and_style/women/the_way_we_live/article4285953.ece Accessed June 2009

Sylvester, R and Thompson, A (2007) Archbishop: pushy parents damaging children. *Daily Telegraph*, 15 September 2007

The United Nations Children's Fund (UNICEF, 2007) *Child Poverty in Perspective: an overview of child wellbeing in rich countries*. Florence: UNICEF Innocenti Research Centre

Walsh, G (2007) Northern Ireland. In Clark, M M and Waller, T (eds) *Early Childhood Education and Care: policy and practice*. London: Sage Publications

Walsh, G and Kehoe, S (2007) *Sesame Tree Northern Ireland: educational objectives and links with the early years curricula*. Report commissioned by New Sesame Workshop, New Jersey

Walsh, G, Sproule, L, McGuiness, C, Trew, K, Rafferty, H and Sheehy, N (2006) An appropriate curriculum for the 4-5 year-old child in Northern Ireland: comparing play-based and formal approaches. *Early Years: An International Journal of Research and Development*, 26(2) p201-221

10

Romanian Childhoods: continuity and change through intergenerational lenses

Horatiu Rusu and Anca Bejenaru

Introduction

Romania is an Eastern European country, now part of the European Union. The population was estimated at over 21 million in 2006. Almost 90 per cent are Romanians, and 85 per cent are orthodox in religion. Approximately 55 per cent of Romanians live in urban areas. The occupational structure of Romania is as follows: approximately 41 per cent in services, 29.7 in agriculture, hunting and fisheries, 23.2 per cent in industry and 6.1 per cent in construction (NIS, 2007). According to the 2002 census, its ethnic structure is 89.5 per cent Romanians, 6.6 Hungarians, 2.5 Rroma, 1.4 other ethnic backgrounds (Germans, Ukrainians, Turks etc).

Like all the former communist countries, Romania began a process of fundamental transformations after the 1989 revolution that entailed: reformation of the political system, changes of legislation, land reform, transfer of state property to private property, educational reform. Probably more than other countries that joined the EU, the transition in Romania encapsulated elements of chaos, desperation and lack of morality, including violent social movements and political and corruption scandals.The political system adopted in 1990 proved to be an original, if ambiguous, combination of a parliamentary system with two chambers and a presidential republic with a five year term of office.

In some respects, for example, high inflation, unemployment, economic in-security, the first decade after the revolution can be called the dark period of post-communism, when Romania had among the poorest performances in its reformation of the economic system of the former communist countries that are now EU members. During this period before 2000 among the greatest problems for Romanians were unemployment, extended poverty and infla-tion. Both the earnings and savings of the people were exposed to devalua-tion because of the explosive rates of inflation (see Rusu, 2008). The economic decline ended in 2000, when the economic sector started to improve and nine years of economic growth followed.

This Chapter analyses changes in the conceptualisation of early childhood in Romania over a period from before the Second World War into the com-munist and post communist era. Our discussion about issues concerning early childhood is based on both objective and subjective indicators. In the first section, the focus is on hard data; the latter contains self representations of childhood, based on interviews.

One image we are trying to capture, concerns the structural changes asso-ciated with early childhood, and derives from a perspective entitled the *politicising of childhood* (see Leira and Saraceno eds, 2008; Ellingsæter and Leira, 2006). This recognises both the role of the family as a primary care environment, and the framing of childhood, 'as a matter of public importance and concern, something for (welfare) state intervention' (Leira and Saraceno eds, 2008:1). We are thus emphasising conceptualisations of childhood re-flected in social and political planning actions (legal and organisational) of the State. This approach raises the problem of the strategic investments a State makes in its citizens, namely the matter of *human capital*, and high-lights two main aspects of public concern, especially referring to children, namely education and health. According to various definitions, human capital is an intangible form of capital, expressing knowledge, ideas, informa-tion, skills, competences, and the health of individuals, which are relevant to economic activity (Schultz, 1971; Becker, 1993 and 2002; Coleman, 1988). The notion of human capital highlights central themes that are of concern in all discussions concerning the nature of childhood (see James and James, 2004; Brannen, 2004). It is a concept that has been popular in communist countries (see also Becker, 1993).

The second dimension of our study considers the family as the primary care environment, with the focus on the experiences people had in their early childhood as reported by different generations.

The research methodology

The study had two aspects, the first quantitative, and the second interview-based and qualitative. The first aspect encompassed the changes in the legislative measures in Romania concerning early childhood and the public response to them. The first quantitative aspect on education and health was based mainly on data from the National Institute of Statistics (NIS 1972, 1986, 1992, 1995, 2007). Apart from being objective measures of a State's level of modernity, these indicators could be interpreted as measuring the relative importance the State gives to early childhood education and health.

Out of the three possible types of education (formal, non-formal and informal) we will look only at the first one and briefly at the last one. The indicators we have studied are: enrolment numbers in nurseries and kindergartens; the number of nurseries and beds in nurseries; number of beds in the State's residential care centres; number of kindergartens and personnel in kindergartens. With regard to the health dimension, the indicator we have considered, due to data availability, is infant mortality rates.

The second type of analysis aims to capture the changes in early childhood through the eyes of the people, that is, the way people construct it. The methodology was inspired by a similar study conducted by Brannen (2004). We used a purposeful sampling strategy, selecting families and members of the families having four generations available to us. A narrative interviewing approach was adopted. The interviews were conducted either on the maternal or paternal line with family members of all generations (great grandparents, grandparents and parents) except the youngest one, where the storyteller was either the father or mother. First the narrators were invited, by means of an initial opening question, and without interruption or further questions, to give a full account of their childhood lives. In the second part, the interviewer initiated more elaborate narrations on salient experiences that appeared in the first part. Finally, the informants were invited to address the issues related to the specific focus of the study where there was not already sufficient detail from the interview. In addition to the two central themes which formed part of our initial analyses, namely education and health, we invited the narrators to explore issues like time use, play, security, household roles.

Structural changes in early education and care

By the end of the nineteenth century, the educational function with regard to early years was entirely in the hands of the families in Romania. Every child was obtaining an education reflecting its primary socialisation environment

(Majuru, 2006). The first attempt to relocate the educational function for children between 3 and 6 to 7 years from the private, family domain, to the public domain, dates from 1881 when the first kindergarten was established. The first law setting up the establishment of the State organisations centred on early years education dates from 1896. In 1910 the first regulation on the internal management of the schools for young children was adopted, stipulating also that the kindergarten be free and compulsory (EACEA, 2009).

The aim of the kindergarten, until 1948, was to offer care and educational opportunities for children whose parents were unable to provide this because of their work, a goal that was far from being attained because most of the families lived in socio-economically deprived environments, especially in rural areas (Majuru, 2006). The numbers of such kindergartens grew continuously, reaching 1,577 units and 90,787 enrolled children by 1938-1939 (NIS, 1972). In spite of this growth, up until 1948-1949 early childhood was still mainly conceptualised in terms of the family's role as provider of care and educator of young children.

The installation of the communist regime, generated after 1947, a massive focus of the State on raising its economic productivity, embodied in an increasing process of excessive industrialisation and forced urbanisation. Urbanisation meant the fragmentation of traditional extended families, and the rise of nuclear families. This structural change in the family deprived the parents of extended family support, especially by grandparents, in caring for and educating the children. Additionally, the communist ideology promoting gender equality, coupled with the pressing need of a second income in the families, caused increasing participation of women in the labour force (Zamfir *et al*, 1999). The integration of women into the labour force and the family policies regulating the return of mothers to work almost immediately after the child's birth (60 days maternity leave) have stimulated the *de-familisation* of childhood. All these developments influenced the conceptualisation of early childhood in the communist era, leading to the establishment of alternative provision for caring for and educating young children. Eventually provision for early childhood entered the public sphere.

The beginning of the communist regime brought the rapid development and institutionalisation of a network of nurseries and kindergartens for children aged 3 months to 6 to 7 years, but the education reform in 1948 eliminated obligatory attendance at the kindergartens. In 1949, Decree 343 established two types of nurseries for children between 3 months and 3 years: daily and weekly nurseries. They were designed primarily as medical services, targeting health care and appropriate nutrition but neglecting educational needs.

The kindergartens, for children between 3 and 7 years of age, were also of two types: daily, those having a normal programme (four hours per day) and weekly, those having an extended programme (eight to ten hours per day). In addition to their primary function of caring for small children, they also had educational roles. The education had rather a collective character, individual needs being reduced to collective needs, aiming ultimately at social homogeneity.

This network of organisations grew continuously up to 1982, increasing in numbers partly because of the rise in the birth rate increase as a consequence of the famous Decree number 770 in 1966 forbidding abortion. For example, the total of 157,934 children enrolled in 2,998 kindergartens in 1948-1949 rose to 935,771 children enrolled in 13,467 kindergartens in 1980-1981. Until 1982, the nurseries and kindergartens were completely free. The economic recession that started in 1982 resulted in a slight change of policies with regard to formal care and education. The medical care, training and education remained free but parents had to finance the costs of food for the children enrolled in kindergartens with the extended programme. As a consequence of extreme poverty and the effects of Decree 770, some families coped with the situation by abandoning their children temporarily or permanently in residential care centres, where the number of beds increased dramatically from 3,311 in 1960, to 13,963 by 1989.

Between 1980 and 1989 a continuous decrease in the number of nurseries and kindergartens is recorded. For example, in 1980 there were registered 902 nurseries, offering 89,130 places, but in 1989 the number decreased to 847 with 77,874 places. A similar situation arose with kindergartens, in 1980-1981 there were 13,467 and by 1988-1989, only 12,169. The kindergartens' personnel followed the same trend: increased between 1939 and 1980 from 1819 to 38,512 and decreased to 31,293 by 1989. Although the quality of the services offered by these organisations diminished, the reduction in kindergarten and children numbers are not due to this but rather to a decrease in the birth rate.

There were few alternatives to the state nurseries or kindergartens (see Kligman, 1998). The luckiest children had grandparents taking care of them up to the school age of 6 or 7 years of age. Another option, valid for the few families having a better than average economic status, was hiring a nanny to take care of the children while the parents were at work. No data are available on which to base an estimate of the extent of this provision.

A consequence of the demographic policies of the communists was the appearance of the phenomenon of the devaluation of children. They were no longer regarded as a blessing for the family, but a source of threat and anxiety (Muntean, 2001). Thus it is easy to understand why one of the first legislative changes after the 1989 revolution was the abrogation of Decree 770. This was followed by a series of policies aiming to revalue the child-parent relationship, and in a way to re-establish the family as the basis of childhood. In this respect, in 1990 paid maternity leave was extended to one year; in 1997 it was extended to two years, both parents qualifying for it since then. An indirect factor that contributed since 1990 to private, family caring and education of young children was, in the transition period, the decrease in the labour force participation rate of working age women (Bădulescu, 2006). Another factor contributing to the reassertion of the centrality of the family's role in childhood was the poor quality of the caring services offered by nurseries to the children aged 0 to 3 years. In the first years of transition no effort was made to develop early childhood services in either urban or rural areas. Therefore, the only public organisations available for the children aged 0 to 3 years remained the nurseries, focused exclusively on caring, targeting health care and appropriate nutrition, but not education.

Until 2005 there were no new educational policies or laws concerning early childhood education, the system working by the same standards as in 1974. The poor quality of the services offered by these nurseries, but also the possibility of the parents taking care of their children up to 2 years of age, resulted in a decrease in the number of centres for young children (0-3 years) from 847 in 1989, to 273 in 2006. In 2005 the first National Strategy for Early Education was outlined. In 2007, under the guidance of the EU, it was adopted as the first law regulating the establishing, organising and functioning of the nurseries: Law 263. In 2008, a national curriculum for early education was released and between 2008 and 2011, several national projects concerning the reform of early education are under way. Associated with the renewed interest in early years education are a series of measures, incentives, and vouchers covering nursery costs, aimed at supporting parents, both in caring for children and their own reintegration into the labour force.

Unlike the nurseries, the kindergarten services profited from a constant improvement after 1989. One cause was the implementation of numerous programmes in this area, including educational alternatives such as Montessori and Step by Step (OECD, 2003). Although the number of public kindergartens suffered a reduction after 1989, from 12,529 in 1990-1991 to 1526 by 2006-2007, a number of private kindergartens were established during this period;

there were none in 1990-1991 but by 2006-2007 (NIS, 2007) there were 194. Nevertheless the high costs of these private kindergartens make them accessible to only a small number of children.

Recently the provision of the last year of kindergarten has become compulsory for children aged 6-7 years and the attendance rate has grown continuously, from 54.3 per cent in 1990-1991 to 76.6 per cent in 2008-2009. At the kindergarten level it seems possible to get closer to the Barcelona targets set by the European Council in 2002 concerning childcare services in EU, namely to enrol 90 per cent of children age 3 to 7 years. However, the target of 33 per cent enrolment in nurseries for children from birth to 3 years of age seems an impossible task, considering that in 2006 the actual enrolment rate was 2.05 per cent.

The health indicators available show a constant improvement. The infant mortality rate of infants under one year of age per one thousand live births reduced from 179 per thousand in 1938 to 116.7 in 1950, and has continued to improve to 15 per thousand by 2005.

Data presented in this section indicate an increasing emphasis by the State on early childhood. This offers the promise of more and more public involvement over what used to be a private matter, educating and caring for young children.

Early childhood through the eyes of the people
Great grandparents' childhood
The seven people interviewed were born between the two world wars and are 76 to 91 years old. Their stories have a lot of similarities, but also some differences between those born around the Great Depression and those born earlier. Most of them lived their childhood in rural areas, and even those living in towns describe a rather rural life. The extended family had the main role in educating the children; none of them attended a kindergarten or nursery. School started for all of them around the age of 7. Health care was provided on intuitive bases, with traditional remedies. It was not uncommon to give birth unattended. Playing in courtyards or in the neighbourhoods was the dominant activity of their early childhood. BA, a great grandmother of 80, recollects: 'we were playing on the street, in the courtyards with other children, all day long. Children that small had nothing else to do.' The games involved the natural surroundings: trees, sticks, mud or water. The toys (dolls or balls) were made out of scraps of cloths or animal hair.

BA: 'We didn't have toys. We made our toys of scraps of cloths ... and swing and dragged them after us because sometimes they were heavier than us.'

Playing in the street was no threat to security. Corporal punishments like being beaten with a wooden stick or a nettle, or being slapped, a frequent theme. Household chores started around age 6 or 7 when children had to take care of domestic animals or participate in agricultural activities like gardening, weeding or hoeing. Up to this age some children were on occasion involved in spinning or in taking care of the chickens: 'by the age of 6 all we did was chasing the chickens'. (BC, 71 years old)

Those born around the Great Depression emphasised more than the others the precarious living conditions: lack of food and clothing, and illnesses. BE, a great grandmother age 77 from a family with six children said:

> What childhood ... there was nothing to do ... there was poverty, we had one room, what to do?... all the children were starving, they were crying of starvation... We lived in misery, o my God how many died of tuberculosis ... repulsive childhood.

Every great grandmother's story we listened to conceptualised their childhood in terms of the family's role as provider of care and as educator.

Grandparents' childhood
Seven grandparents, aged 59 to 66 were interviewed. Their early childhood stories are fairly similar. Everyone lived their childhood in town. During the summer they spent their holidays with their grandparents in villages. Everyone attended kindergarten for at least two years. AB, a 66-years-old woman describes the kindergarten:

> There were a lot of children ... boys and girls altogether. We had toys, pinafores and slippers. We use to eat at ten. There was a swing in the courtyard.

The family still played an important role in education, most children attending a four hours daily programme. To quote AC, 63 years old:

> Everyone got his education from his parents in first place ... we were taught not to lie, steal, or misbehave ... to be civilised.

The road to kindergarten was safe. Professional health care was available: 'when we got sick, we were going to doctors' (AD, 59 years old). Playing in courtyards or in the neighbourhood was an important activity. 'I was playing in the courtyard ... with more than fifteen kids of different ages' (AE, 66 years old). Nobody remembers having many toys at home. The neighbourhood was safe. Corporal punishment still existed, but was not much invoked. House-hold chores were not an issue.

Mothers and children

The mothers are aged 31 to 38. Everyone spent their childhood in town and attended kindergarten at least for one year; some also attended nurseries. An authoritarian pedagogy prevailed:

> the system was much more severe, we didn't have the liberty our children have today ... I consider it was better. (PA, age 31, curator)

The main activities in kindergarten were drawing, making collages, singing, learning short poems and playing. The roads to kindergarten were safe. Children were integrated as early as kindergarten into a communist organisation called 'Motherland's Hawks' which was supposed to offer a non-formal education according to the communist ethos. The medical system was well developed, everyone in need benefiting from healthcare. As some recollect, milk, cheese and meat were scarce and they joined their parents or grandparents to queue for hours to buy them. They used to play in the streets in summer and indoors in winter: 'we had no internet, no electronic games and few TV programmes' (PB, age 33, journalist). The neighbourhood was considered safe. Corporal punishment, such as striking the hand with a ruler or spoon, was seldom applied at home.

The children are 2 to 7 years old, and all attend or will attend kindergarten (state or private). They are seen as having many more opportunities. Kindergarten education is considered adequate: 'the educators are well trained ... but the children are more pretentious.' (PB, age 31, nurse) Nurseries are attended by some children, especially in those cases where no extended family support is nearby and the parents cannot afford a nanny, even though they are not a good option for children. As PA (age 31, curator) observes:

> My friends who put their children in nurseries are permanently facing health problems because they are not properly cared for even though the infrastructure exists.

Most of the children are integrated into their family's daily activities through routine activities, such as cleaning, cooking or gardening. The grandparents have, in some cases, an important role in taking care of children while the parents are at work. In other cases children attend the eight hour programme kindergarten. Playing at home involves commercial toys and watching television: 'Winnie the Pooh, and cars, animal toys, Lego'. (PC, 31, insurance agent) Playing with other children seems to happen seldom, because the parents are too involved in work, and other daily activities. Neighbourhoods and streets are no longer considered safe playgrounds. Quasi permanent surveillance is present when the children are outside the house. No corporal punishments are applied: punishments consist in forbidding different activities. Long term health and safety of the children preoccupies the parents, some of them setting up stem cell stocks or private insurance for their children.

The stories we have summarised here are complementary to the structural evolution described earlier. Family as a primary care environment is gradually supplemented or even replaced by the nursery and kindergarten system. The latter is perceived more and more as a must. The time dedicated to unrestricted play activities seems to be decreasing. Playing daily with many children, on the streets, is gradually being replaced, due to concern about security in the neighbourhood, with playing from time to time with a few friends, in arranged playgrounds, or alone, watching TV, or playing in kindergarten. Immediate health concerns are no longer an issue, instead, health and social security concerns are projected towards the longer term.

Conclusions

Our analysis was dedicated to the intergenerational changes concerning early childhood. The main issue was the balance between the family role as a primary care environment and public interest and support in educating and caring for children. Issues were inspected over four generations: human capital issues and issues like time use, play, security, household roles. Our data indicate that the changes in early childhood are moving gradually from private concern to public concern, from survival issues to welfare issues.

The role of formal and non-formal education has increased significantly. We have observed the willingness of parents to invest in their children, as more children of 3 years of age or younger attend extracurricular training. The time spent by children in the family is becoming shorter and shorter, in favour of time spent in supervised, specialised environments. In this context, services for the socialisation, recreation, education and health of children have experienced a boom in recent years.

An important final aspect is the new emphasis in Romania on children's rights, especially after the entry into force of new legislation in January 2005. For the first time, the Romanian legislation truly reflects children's rights as stipulated in the UN Convention on the Rights of the Child (United Nations, 1989).

Points for discussion

◼ In what important ways have the lives of young children in Romania changed in recent years?

◼ What problems will recent changes present to parents and early years practitioners?

References

Bădulescu, A (2006). Şomajul în România. O analiză retrospectivă (1991-2005). *Economie teoretică şi aplicată* 2 p71-76

Becker G S (1993) *Human Capital: a theoretical and empirical analysis with special reference to education.* Third Edition. Chicago: University of Chicago Press

Becker, G S (2002) The Age of Human Capital. In Lazear, E P (ed) *Education in the Twenty-First Century.* Palo Alto: Hoover Institution Press

Brannen, J (2004) Childhoods across the generations. Stories from women in four-generation English families. *Childhood.* 11(4) p409-428

Coleman, J S (1988) Social Capital in the Creation of Human Capital. *The American Journal of Sociology.* 94 p95-120

EACEA (2009). *Organizarea sistemului educaţional în România* 2007/08. EACEA, Eurydice: Brussels

Ellingsæter, A L and Leira, A (2006). *Politicising Parenthood in Scandinavia: gender relations in welfare states.* Bristol: The Policy Press

James A and James A L (2004) *Constructing childhood: theory, policy and social practice.* London: Palgrave Macmillan

Kligman, G (1998) *The Politics of Duplicity: controlling reproduction in Ceausescu's Romania.* Berkeley, University of California Press

Leira, A and Saraceno, C (eds) (2008) *Childhood: Changing Contexts.* Bingley: Emerald Group Publishing

Majuru, A (2006) *Copilăria la români.* Bucuresti, Editura Compania

Muntean, A (2001) *Familii si copii in dificultate.* Timişoara, Editura Mirton

National Institute of Statistics (NIS) *Romanian Statistical Yearbooks* (1972, 1975,1986, 1992, 1995, 2007). Bucureşti: National Institute of Statistics Publishing

OECD (2003). *Europe du Sud-Est. FYROM, Moldavie, Monténégro, Roumanie, Serbie – Volume 2.* OECD Publishing

Rusu, Horaţiu (2008) *Schimbare socială şi identitate socioculturală.* Iaşi: Polirom

Schultz, T W (1971) *Investment in Human Capital: the role of education and of research.* New York: Free Press

United Nations (1989) *Convention on the Rights of the Child.* Geneva: UN

Zamfir, E, Zamfir, C and Cace, S (1999) *Politici de suport pentru femei.* In Zamfir, C (ed.) *Politici sociale în România.* Bucureşti: Expert

Websites

European Council (2002). Presidency Conclusion. Barcelona European Council 15 and 16 March 2002 http://www.consilium.europa.eu/ueDocs/cms_Data/docs/pressData/en/ec/71025.pdf Accessed October 2009

Ministerul Educaţiei, Cercetării şi Inovării (2005). *Strategie privind educaţia timpurie* (ET). http://www.edu.ro/index.php?module=uploads&func=download&fileId=2416 Accessed October 2009

11

Weaving a New Life: a Somali family's resettlement in urban America

Lynne Williamson

Contributions from Fatuma Ahmed and Mohamed Adan, based on oral history interviews form the basis for this Chapter.

Introduction

Imagine boarding a giant plane for somewhere you can barely imagine, never having seen television, the internet or a phone. You are allowed one suitcase, not a problem because your possessions won't fill it. You desperately want to escape from your current situation, but rumours about the new destination terrify you. It is hot in Kenya where you have been living for fourteen years. What will the temperature be like where you are headed? Who will be there to meet you? How will you know where to go, and has someone organised a place for you to sleep? There are nine of you, one child barely walking – how will you all find food? Will people harass you because you are Muslim? Will you ever get over your longing for your own country? Will you ever feel comfortable in the new place? Will there be a hopeful future for you there?

This situation, faced by a family originally from Somalia but held in a refugee camp in Kenya for over a decade, is very common as aid organisations, faith-based groups, and political entities resettle large populations displaced by wars and ethnic violence. In the United States, 53,738 refugees entered in 2005, the year Fatuma Ahmed and her eight children came to America. Two hundred and forty-five Somali refugees arrived in Connecticut during that year, out of a total of 526 refugees from several countries (Administration for

Children and Families, 2005). Fatuma's long journey from rural Somalia to inner city Hartford, and her family's story of successful transition, illuminates the social, political, cultural and emotional struggles faced by refugees as they build new lives.

Life in a Kenyan refugee camp

The grim story of Somali refugees in Kenyan holding camps remains largely unknown in the West. Interviews with Fatuma and her eldest son Mohamed Adan in September 2009 offer a harrowing glimpse into conditions borne by families, especially children, in the camps. Somalia has experienced a complex and continuous civil war among rival clans since 1991, in addition to longstanding armed conflict with Ethiopia, leading to violence, famine and dislocation for hundreds of thousands of Somalis. Most of these refugees have fled to Kenya, where the United Nations High Commission for Refugees (UNHCR) in collaboration with international humanitarian organisations has maintained camps for displaced Somalis. The three camps in Dadaab housed 127,390 refugees in 2005, Fatuma's family included (UNHCR, 2009).

Fatuma Ahmed, along with her farmer husband and five young sons, belonged to the Ashraf, a Somali minority group often targeted by larger armed clans fighting for power. Along with thousands of others, the family fled across country on donkeys and camels, arriving in Kenya in 1992. The boys ranged in age from 7 to newborn, and Fatuma was pregnant with her daughter. Although safe from the violence in Somalia, prejudices and chaos transferred to the camps.

> We had problems with other Somalis in the camps, there was not that much rule and we were persecuted. You are attacked and beaten up, you can't do anything, many times it happened to us; three or four children will beat your child up, you can't fight back. If you get into trouble there is no one to help you. (Adan, 2009)

The family existed on maize and basic rations distributed by relief agencies. Each family dug its own latrine with few tools. Diseases such as tuberculosis and severe diarrhoea became endemic. Fatuma would walk outside the camp to collect firewood; carrying heavy loads back to the camp for cooking and to sell to others for a few shillings, to buy additional food such as tomatoes and onions. The family gathered grass for their one sheep and one goat, selling any extra to others. They built their own shelter out of tree branches and cow dung. Although she had not gone to school in Somalia, Fatuma was skilled at handwork, making woven sisal mats that brought some income in the camps.

Fatuma's husband had returned to Somalia, and did not rejoin the family in Kenya for seven years; he married again and had several children in Somalia.

Carrying the firewood caused headaches that plague Fatuma even today. She fell ill, and Mohamed took on the cooking and support of the younger children. The family now included eight children, three born in the camps after occasional visits from the father.

> Mom got sick, she suffered a lot, doing too much work, stress, by herself with little children ... I was working at the age of 12, bringing money to the family. I was in school but on Fridays I would take a wheelbarrow and carry the food people got from the distribution center. I negotiated the price with them, then carried their food. I was very healthy then and worked hard but it was really hot and I was barefoot. (Adan, 2009)

Social conditions in the camp were terrifying.

> Gangs in the camp – during the night they come to your home and ask you to give them everything. If you don't do it, they will kill you and take it. They didn't do this to us because we didn't have anything to loot! Maybe even your neighbours would do this if they think you have money. Women get raped every day, because they have to collect firewood from outside. The bandits see them and go after them, also disfigure with knives. They torture the men in the houses at night. Next day you may recognise them, but the only choice is to look down or else they will come and kill you. Many people were killed like that, many, many.

> You can't survive there; your situation is not changing. We can't go back to Somalia because of the war still going on, we can't stay in Kenya because we don't belong there, we belong nowhere. (Adan, 2009)

All the older brothers attended schools run by UNHCR and the camp agencies. Mohammed was in Form Three (11th grade) in 2005, holding the third or fourth position in his class. If he had maintained that ranking he would have won a free scholarship and full family resettlement to Canada, but the family left Kenya before the scholarship exam.

In 2004, after years of seeing hopes for resettlement dashed, Ashraf Somalis were selected for relocation as UNHCR stepped up efforts to protect Somali minority groups. The approval process took thirteen months of interviews with UNHCR, health agencies, and US Homeland Security. The family went to Nairobi for orientation, then boarded a regular commercial flight to Amsterdam with three other Somali families, all wearing uniforms that identified them as refugees in transit. Their next destination was New York City, on the way to Connecticut.

Arrival in Hartford

Due in part to its proximity to New York as a major entry point and its favourable job market, Connecticut's immigrant and refugee population has grown rapidly. Hartford's population in 2000 included 18.6 per cent foreign-born individuals; with 46.5 per cent speaking languages other than English at home (State and County Quick Facts, 2009). Over one hundred ethnic groups live in the city, with more than fifty non-English languages spoken in schools and ten per cent of the population who are recent immigrants (Education World, 2006). About 17.4 per cent of students in Hartford schools are enrolled as English Language Learners (Connecticut State Department of Education, 2009). The city's largest ethnicities are Latino from several Spanish-speaking groups, African American, and Caribbean American, comprising 78.5 per cent of the population (State and County Quick Facts, 2009). In 2007, 31.2 per cent of Hartford's residents live below the poverty level (Advameg, 2009); the child poverty rate is 47 per cent (Commission on Children, 2009).

Fatuma and her family arrived into this ethnic mix and stressed economic environment in September 2005. After landing at New York City Airport, and being processed by the Immigration and Naturalisation Service, they spent their first night alone in a Manhattan staging house.

> We had orientation in Nairobi, told what to expect but you don't know if it will be true, what strangers are with you who could take you anywhere, we had heard stories too about people who will rob you, cut your heart out. In New York we had beds and a phone, but we didn't know how to use a phone or what a phone was! (Adan, 2009)

In the morning a driver picked them up and headed for Hartford, about three hours away. This man was helpful and experienced with refugees, and Mohamed recalls his kindness as a tremendous relief. The family was met in Hartford by a caseworker from Catholic Charities, a Somali man who spoke to them in their own language and drove them to their apartment. The caseworker assured them that they would meet other Somalis and everything would work out well. It had been three days since leaving Nairobi, a time of total disorientation, fear, and new experiences.

Hungerford Street: the first three years

Located on the edge of Hartford's Latino neighbourhood and within view of the State Capitol, Hungerford Street represents a difficult residential environment. Most of the multi-family buildings are rented by often unscrupulous absentee landlords. Constructed in the early twentieth century, the buildings have housed generations of immigrants. Resettlement agencies arrange apartments there for recently-arrived families because the rents are relatively low and the apartments accommodate large families. The buildings show their age and the general neglect of the landlords. Bedbugs and rats abound. Drugs are openly sold in the parking lots. However, the street appeals to Muslim newcomers because one of Hartford's three mosques is located there. Fatuma was pleased to discover that another Somali family lived nearby, people she had known in the camps. This family became Fatuma's main social support during her first month in America.

Still, adjusting to the realities of an American city took a great deal of inner strength and persistence. Catholic Charities Migration and Refugee Services assisted with finding and furnishing the apartment, obtaining Social Security cards, registering the children with schools, arranging inoculations and food stamps, applying for Connecticut Department of Social Services (DSS) benefits, and more. Usually, once those initial elements are in place, the agency becomes less involved and the post-resettlement process begins. Mohamed felt that the family was left on its own to navigate through the often impenetrable red tape and social service jargon.

> Caseworkers or DSS, they pretend to help but no one calls back. But we learned quickly – when a letter comes in the mail we can read it without having to ask someone to read for us, because you don't know if that person is lying to you. If you wait for your case worker, it might take days and you might miss an appointment that was in the letter. (Adan, 2009)

The other Somali family, involved with jobs and school and the pressure of their own acclimation, also became less available to help. Without a car the family's ability to obtain necessities, keep their health appointments, and travel to jobs was limited. Mohamed fell in the snow while walking to work one day, requiring surgery on his back. While a bus system does exist in Hartford, grocery and other stores are distant and not always located directly on the bus line. In larger shopping areas surrounded by highways, sidewalks are non-existent. Prices at small neighborhood stores are expensive and the food choice limited. The problem of access to nutritional food choices in inner-city neighborhoods remains severe. For families used to a completely different diet, understanding American food proved bewildering. 'The refrigerator is full of food, but who knows what it is?' (Adan, 2009)

The mosque played a central role in helping the family to settle into the neighborhood. Fatuma's older sons Mohamed and Abdi were welcomed by an American black Muslim man.

As soon as he met us he took us to the mosque and we prayed there. We were very joyful when we went there because we thought we would not meet any Muslims since this is not a Muslim country. We feared we would not see any mosques anymore ... We were happy to see so many people who said don't worry you'll be fine.

Other social contacts for Mohamed and Abdi included a Nigerian on Hungerford Street who had lived in America for seventeen years, and a Somali businessman, Ali, who befriended the family and served as a vital conduit to information and assistance. He gave Fatuma bags of supplies from his store, drove the older sons to stores and offices, taught them how to use computers and read the newspaper, introduced them to many resources, and helped them navigate the city. Ali negotiated with the Board of Education to permit Abdi to enter Hartford High School, and enrolled Mohamed in adult education classes. 'So we start learning, through people around, asking questions, walking around, going to the mosque a lot. We learned from the other Muslim community and Somalis.' (Adan, 2009)

Ali also stepped in when the family needed legal help. Seemingly friendly and helpful, their African American landlady drove Fatuma to a grocery store on two occasions to buy food. She showed Fatuma how to pay with the food stamp card by swiping it through the credit machine. Only after Ali checked the register receipt against the groceries in the house did he realise that the landlady had taken half of the food for herself. After being confronted with this deception, the landlady's relationship with the family deteriorated badly. She refused to fix serious structural problems in the apartment, and her husband harassed Fatuma when he came to collect the rent. Finally the family was evicted illegally.

A move to the suburbs

In addition to housing problems, the younger children were being bullied in Hartford elementary schools. The oldest daughter, now 15, was targeted by Latina girls on the school bus because of her headscarf. She would fight back but then be disciplined by the principal. This daughter chose to walk to school, a distance of over a mile, leading to frostbite in her toes during one winter. Her learning in school suffered as did her emotional health. In August 2008 the family moved to a housing project in Windsor, a suburban town six miles north of Hartford. The rent for their small apartment is high and Fatuma finds it difficult to travel to Hartford for her English classes at the Library due to less frequent buses. However the progress made by the children socially and educationally has been remarkable. The oldest daughter in

particular improved her English to complete fluency, and she wins certifi-
cates for academic achievement. She enjoys a wide circle of friends, and has
adjusted well to life in a smaller town. The two youngest children attend after-
school programmes at the mosque in Windsor. The family considers the
move a success.

A central factor in Fatuma's growing confidence comes from her involvement
in an arts enterprise that encourages and supports her abilities as a crafts-
woman. The Connecticut folk arts programme, part of a national network of
similar initiatives, provides technical assistance for artists with knowledge of
cultural traditions and art forms. The programme director met Fatuma in
2007 and has encouraged her production of handwoven Somali bags and
baskets. Fatuma has joined traditional weavers, lace makers, and em-
broiderers from several immigrant groups as part of the Sewing Circle Project
established by the author (Williamson, 2008). The women meet weekly at the
Hartford Public Library to share their techniques, develop product ideas, and
collaborate on marketing opportunities. They sell their work at farmers'
markets, craft fairs and marketplaces. Fatuma has been particularly successful with sales of her baskets, and welcomes the extra income. She derives an
equal benefit from the camaraderie of the other artisans as well as from
regular exposure to American audiences. Fatuma's English language facility,
her financial acumen and her comfort in self-expression have all improved
through this programme. In addition, her basket-making reminds Fatuma of
Somali cultural practices, and provides a way to contribute her personal skills
to American cultural life.

In September 2009, four years after arriving in Hartford, Mohamed flew to
Kenya to marry a woman selected for him by his father. The 18-year-old
woman comes from an Eyle clan family with strong Muslim values; she is the
daughter of Mohamed's father's best friend in the camps. Mohamed will
return to the US without his wife, but will begin family reunification paper-
work to bring her to Hartford as soon as possible. He will look for housing that
will accommodate the two nuclear families in separate but nearby apartments, either in Windsor or Hartford. Like many parents, the family's primary
concern is locating good schools where the children can learn in a supportive
and safe environment. They would like the children to attend Hartford's
recently developed Magnet Schools, believing that these theme-based educational environments promise more serious learning than other schools. The
combination of appropriate, affordable housing and high-quality schools will
determine the family's choice of where to live. Fatuma wants to stay in Connecticut, despite their rocky start. She has heard positive stories from Somalis

who have relocated to other states such as Ohio and Maine, but her social network in Greater Hartford, her English and computer classes at the Hartford Public Library, her Sewing Circle friends, her basket-making accomplishments, sustain her emotionally. The family's stability and her children's achievements in their education settings are important factors in Fatuma's choice to stay in Connecticut, despite the cold winters. 'If my children are happy, I am happy! I like Connecticut! I like to stay in Connecticut! ' (Ahmed, 2009)

The future

All of the older brothers have jobs, with all but one intent on going to college and developing careers while living in Windsor with Fatuma. Abdi is enrolled in a university course in mechanical engineering, having won several school awards and gaining a full scholarship; he will probably go on for an advanced degree. Mohamed will soon complete an associate's degree in computer information systems then transfer to a four-year college to study computer engineering. His consistently high marks qualify him for Phi Beta Kappa, a national academic honor society that offers scholarships. He will also continue to work full-time and look after the family.

> College will take longer to finish, because I will have to work outside and will have to drive my family, to help my Mom and children. I have to accept the responsibility of the family because if I am in school all the time then my family will suffer. (Adan, 2009)

One casualty of relocation to America has been the language facility of the younger children. The six older children speak both MaayMaay and Somali, but Hassan (age 12) and Felhada (age 7) have almost lost these, since English is increasingly the language of the home. This distresses Fatuma, who tries to preserve the children's Somali while she herself struggles to learn English. She also monitors closely the children's acculturation to American ways, their dress, food, friends, outside activities, and television viewing. The older brothers encourage the children to maintain traditional practices as much as possible, drive them to the mosque, and support their school activities.

> There's a Somali proverb – whatever the big camel does, the small camel will do too! Even though some of my younger brothers are not the way we want them – if they are more Americanised and they are not doing the right way, me and my next brother we treat them good and show them the right way, we tell them the truth, we help them out so they don't have to suffer, then they know and grow up in a good way. Even if we are poor and we struggle around, at

least they see what we do. We tell them how good it is to do well on your own – do your homework; don't watch this stuff you see on the TV, it's just stories don't believe it. So the younger boys, they are smart – they already know what drugs are, they know the difference already. We tell them if you go the wrong way, you will just suffer and you will have nothing. (Adan, 2009)

Fatuma herself has achieved a measure of independence and contentment despite constant concerns about financial security. It seems unlikely that her husband will join her, since he now has a second family in Kenya. Fatuma's focus remains on her children, and her hoped-for role as a grandmother.

Reflections

Fatuma and Mohamed have shown extraordinary personal strength through-out their long journey. The stories quoted here, as well as others emerging during our interviews, illustrate their willingness to take advantage of every opportunity, to make definite choices even when fearful, to take chances and fail, and learn from all experiences. These characteristics are shared by the entire family, and have contributed to their construction of a hopeful new life in a challenging environment.

At the beginning it was very scary because we didn't know what we know now, that we would succeed. What's going to happen? We need a car, we need a phone, we need everything, we need money, school It turned out in a good way – we get some support from the state for Mom, because of the younger kids we get food stamps. We live with them, we add some money for rent, we help pay bills, and if the kids need something we help. We learned the system, we know about the law of the country, so we know which way to go if it comes to education, credit, dealing with the money system, things like that. Dealing with the community, getting a car, now we seem like we are not very new here! (Adan, 2009)

Clearly the other newcomer groups in Hartford have been a source of crucial information and support as Fatuma's family adjusted to life in this city. The Muslim community in particular has provided a deep level of practical and emotional sustenance.

In our religion you have to help people not because of blood, but for the sake of humanity. No matter whether he is Jewish, or Christian – as long as the person is a human being, our religion states that you have to be helpful to him. Mom was the best Mom we could ever have imagine, in the camps she didn't get any help, there is no government, nobody to do anything ... I expected to grow up [as a child] in Kenya, but after Mom got sick, I became a man, I was responsible. Mom tells me you are doing what even a parent doesn't do. That's how the little ones survived, through God and through Mom and me. (Adan, 2009).

Resilient families such as Fatuma's identify cultural traditions, including faith, language, arts, and personal and community history, as vitally important for sustaining the health and wellbeing of their group and especially their children. At the same time, they believe that engaging with a wider public is an effective strategy for alleviating issues of conflict or prejudice, and for educating others about their heritage. They hope to develop positive paths towards both integration and cultural preservation. While there have been organisations and programmes along the way that have assisted with these urgent priorities, Fatuma Ahmed and her family have forged their own path to a great extent, wherever they have lived.

Points for discussion

- Consider what important features of Fatima's family enabled them to integrate so successfully into urban life in America.
- What did the local support networks and individuals in the community contribute, and what lessons can be learnt by other communities receiving refugees?

References

Adan, Mohamed (2009) Recorded interview with the author, 16 September

Administration for Children and Families (2005) Fiscal year 2005 refugee arrivals. Washington DC: Health and Human Services, Office of Refugee Resettlement http://www.acf.hhs.gov/programs/orr/data/fy2005RA.htm Accessed November 2009

Advameg, Inc (2009) Hartford (CT) poverty rate data.http://www.city_data.com/poverty/poverty_Hartford_Connecticut.html Accessed November 2009

Ahmed, Fatuma (2009) Interview with the author, 18 November

Commission on Children (2009) Child poverty in Connecticut: January 2009. Hartford: State of Connecticut General Assembly http://www.cga.ct.gov/coc/PDFs/poverty/child_poverty_report_0109.pdf Accessed November 2009

Connecticut State Department of Education (2009) Connecticut's English language learners. http:www.csde.state.ct.us/public/cedar/ell/index Accessed November 2009

Education World (2006) A look at Hartford and its schools. http://www.education_world.com/a_issues/teamingup/teamingup001b.shtml Accessed November 2009

State and County Quick Facts (2009) Hartford (city), Connecticut. Washington DC: US Census Bureau http://quickfacts.census.gov/qfd/states/09/0937000.html Accessed November 2009

UNHCR (2009) Country operations profile, Kenya. http://www.unhcr.org/cgi_bin/texis/vtx/page?page=49e483a16 Accessed November 2009

Williamson, L (2008) Connecticut Cultural Heritage Arts Program sewing circle project. http://www.ctheritagearts.org/index.php?id=64 Accessed November 2009

Section IV
Who Cares?

The focus in this section is on young children whose family circumstances place them at risk of physical or emotional abuse or of neglect. This is a topical and emotive issue, attracting numerous headlines. Professionals are criticised either for intervening too soon; for delay in removing children from their birth parents; or for returning the children to their parents with tragic consequences.

The illustrative material in both Chapters is taken from urban areas, Chapter 12 traces the lives of young children in the West Midlands in the 1960s who were removed from their family and placed with members of the extended family or with foster parents. Chapter 13 describes a very different approach in Glasgow in 2009, whereby vulnerable families are supported and kept together through the work of multidisciplinary teams who aim to transform the family dynamics.

- As you read these Chapters, consider the strengths and weaknesses of these two approaches.
- Investigate the attitude to such issues in your own country and the extent to which current legislation in different parts of the United Kingdom, or in your country, enables various professionals to cooperate in supporting such families.
- Make a note as you read of those whose involvement is necessary if vulnerable children are to be protected and supported?
- What implications does each approach have for the training of practitioners?
- What additional problems might be faced by the families were they to live in rural areas?

12

The Changing Face of Care for Looked After Children in England

Allison Tatton

Introduction

'A nation's greatness is measured by how it treats its weakest members.'

The above quote, or similar, has been attributed to numerous politicians, religious leaders and orators from Aristotle to Gandhi, yet the Department for Children Schools and Families (DCSF, 2008) reports that in England, in the twelve months prior to 31 March 2007, 545,000 children were referred to Social Services Departments: 44 per cent of these referrals were categorised as relating to neglect, 23 per cent were because of emotional abuse and 15 per cent as a result of physical abuse, most at the hands of their parents or carers (Brandon *et al*, 2008). The DCSF report states that referrals have fluctuated between 550,000 and 570,000 per annum in recent years.

The high profile cases of Victoria Climbie, Khyra Ishaq and, more recently Baby P have been well publicised in the media in the United Kingdom. But these children are only the tip of the iceberg. Between March 2003 and March 2005, 161 children in England died or were seriously harmed at the hands of their parents or carers through neglect or abuse, equating to more than one child each week. Of these 47 per cent were reported to be under the age of one year; 83 per cent of all of the children were previously known to children's services (Brandon *et al*, 2008). Brandon *et al*, (2008) also report that, in many of these circumstances, parents or carers were hostile to agency workers, many families moved house many times and there was often a history of alcohol or substance abuse. The question of whether to support the family or remove the child is still of concern.

At any time in England there are approximately 45,000 children being looked after by local authorities. This figure has reduced from a high of over 125,000 in 1946 (Cunningham, 2006) and 70,000 in 1969 (Home Office, 1969). Berridge (1997) claims, however, that while the number of children in care has fluctuated, the number of children in foster care has remained more or less constant over several decades, at around 32,000.

The Chapter explores the changing face of care for looked after children in England. Drawing on largely historical data it provides an overview of the experiences faced by children and their families and the dilemmas encountered by those working within a public care system. It poses important questions such as when is it appropriate to keep a family together or remove a child for its own safety and welfare? It points to a range of enduring debates about what kind of public care system is likely to deliver the best outcomes for children. Although the case study material is English in its origins, the issues raised have a much wider purchase in terms of their consideration of child and parent rights, how different forms of state intervention can have powerful and lasting impact on children's lives and the ethical implications attached to such interventions.

Background

Although names and some places within this Chapter have been changed to preserve anonymity, it is based on the real life experiences of one family in the West Midlands spanning four decades beginning in the late 1940s. Their experiences will be used to highlight the issues that were pertinent then and are still relevant within the care system today. Changes in the care system over recent years will be highlighted and existing weaknesses will be explored.

The 1960s and 1970s marked a period of change for children who were looked after by the State in England. The Curtis Report (1946) recommended that Children's Departments were set up in every Local Authority and the subsequent Children Act 1948 saw this come to fruition, to support children who were deprived of a normal home life (Chase *et al*, 2006). Although preventative work was performed as early as the 1950s, many child care officers had to campaign for the right to be able to spend money on prevention, and in 1963 legislation (1963 Children and Young Persons Act) made it a duty for Local Authorities to promote the welfare of children through this approach (Hendrick, 2005). This was the beginning of more formal family support and intervention. In 1970 Children's Departments were subsumed into Social Services Departments.

The Wright family

The parents were Edward and Josephine Wright. Edward was born in Birmingham in 1924 and his wife Josephine in 1923. The couple were married shortly after the war in 1945. Both Edward and Josephine were considered to be mentally subnormal, a phrase used to describe people who had significant learning difficulties. They had been born into fairly affluent and supportive families; Edward's family owned a manufacturing business in Birmingham and Josephine's family had owned a gentleman's outfitters on the south side of Birmingham. While the couple appeared able to fend for themselves, it soon became apparent that Edward and Josephine found it difficult to settle in one location and they were regularly evicted or moved home of their own accord. Both Josephine and Edward were alcoholics.

Their first child, a daughter Madeline, was born shortly after their marriage in 1946. It was soon apparent to family members that all was not well and that the parents lacked the necessary skills to care for her. Shortly after she was born, their family suggested that Madeline be looked after by Josephine's parents; to this the couple agreed. In 1947, Edward and Josephine had a second child, Jane. Shortly after Jane's birth she was diagnosed with epilepsy and as she grew up it became apparent that she also had severe learning difficulties. As with their first child, Edward and Josephine struggled to look after her. With Jane there was also the added responsibility of having to administer life saving medication. Shortly after her diagnosis, Jane went to live with Edward's mother who was by then a widow. Peter, their third child, was born four years later in 1951. Again, after an initial period when Edward and Josephine tried to look after him with significant family support, it became clear that this was not going to be successful and Josephine's brother and his wife, who were childless, asked if they could adopt Peter. The couple agreed.

A period of six years elapsed before Edward and Josephine had any further children, by which time they were living in a leafy Birmingham suburb and appeared relatively settled. Their fourth child, Elizabeth, was born in 1957. With family support, Edward and Josephine looked after Elizabeth until Josephine became pregnant with their fifth child in early 1959. This pregnancy was not an easy one. Again the situation began to deteriorate. Elizabeth, who was then nearly 2 years old, went to live with Edward's brother.

Edward and Josephine did occasionally see all of their children; not so much in the role of parents but more like a distant uncle and aunt. Although the children were all aware that Edward and Josephine were their parents, there was no attempt on the part of their parents to build or maintain a relationship with them. When they visited, Josephine and Edward appeared to be desirous rather of maintaining a relationship with their own siblings, and showed no special affection towards their own children. There was never any attempt to make contact on special occasions such as birthdays or at Christmas.

Up until this point, all Edward and Josephine's children had thus been sub-sumed into their wider family and they were not known to what was then known as the Children's Department and which in 1970 merged with Social Services.

As can be seen, members of the extended family were able to provide for the first four of Edward and Josephine's children. Taylor (2006) states that of the approximately 61,000 children who are looked after in England and Wales, about 7,000 are looked after by members of the close or extended family.

Edward and Josephine went on to have three more children. Anne was born in 1959, Geraldine in 1962 and Brian in 1964. However, in late 1963, the then two youngest children, Geraldine and Anne, were found in a workman's hut under a flyover in inner city Birmingham. Geraldine was approximately 11 months old and Anne was 3 years and one month. The children, while reasonably well nourished and cared for, had been left alone in the hut while Edward and Josephine went in search of alcohol at a nearby public house. The family had recently been evicted from their property a few miles away and had taken refuge in the hut, where they were living. It is unclear who found them, though it may have been the workmen returning to carry out main-tenance on the flyover. The Children's Department was contacted and Geraldine and Anne were taken into local authority care. The two girls were taken to a children's home in Birmingham, where they lived for about four years.

At the time these children were taken into care, very young children might normally have expected to be placed in residential nurseries which catered for children under 5 years of age, However, the childcare officer in charge of their case, thought it important to place the sisters together. As Geraldine was only 11 months old at the time she was taken into care, she was the youngest of over twenty children who lived in the home with a house mother and house father and numerous staff. Geraldine was considered to be the baby of the family and, as such, felt she received special treatment although there was no concept, at this time of a key worker system. She developed into a healthy and happy child. The older of the two children fared somewhat less favourably. She became very anxious and withdrawn, began biting her nails, preferred to spend long periods of time alone and was regularly found crying by staff.

While they were in the children's home, there were attempts by the family to maintain contact. The aunt who was looking after their older sister, Elizabeth, requested that she be allowed to care for the children. However, her request was refused on the grounds that their house would be overcrowded. The children's older siblings occasionally visited the two girls in the home and on a few occasions the girls were taken to their aunt's house.

Upon the birth of the youngest child, Brian, he was removed from Edward and Josephine and placed in a local authority residential nursery where he stayed until he was 4-years-old. At this point he was fostered with a view to adoption by an affluent couple living in a local suburb. This couple had a son of their own who was 12 months older than Brian. This placement broke down within twelve months. By this time, the girls were being fostered by Mr and Mrs Baker and Brian went to live with his two older sisters.

The foster family

Mr and Mrs Baker had married in 1958 and had two children of their own. They began fostering in the mid 1960s. They had had a succession of short and medium term foster children. In 1966 they had been asked to care for a child from an ethnic minority group who was then 10 months old and in 1968 they were contacted by the Children's Department and asked to consider fostering the two sisters. Following a short period of introduction and transition the girls went to live with Mr and Mrs Baker. In 1969 they were asked to consider also looking after the girls' brother Brian, to which they agreed, again after a short introduction period. The children remained with Mr and Mrs Baker, fostered on a long term basis until their parents died when they were adopted. All of the children at this point were nearing adulthood.

Prior to 1948, fostering was seen as a form of substitute parenting, but the Children Act (1948) changed this so that fostering could be seen as a temporary arrangement to meet the needs of children and parents. However, far beyond 1948 many foster carers still saw fostering as substitute parenting, and often exclusive forms of fostering were practised by some carers, thus shutting out the family of origin from the child's life (Triseloitis, 2004). Long term fostering has sometimes been seen as a failure of the agencies as the aim should be that children are either returned to their parents or adopted. Triseloitis and Hill (1987) point out that children fostered on a long term basis often become integrated into the foster family, yet there was still a degree of uncertainty and insecurity on both the part of the children and the foster parents.

The childcare officer clearly believed that it was desirable to place the two girls together and later to place their younger brother with them, however, there was less importance placed on maintaining contact with their parents or other siblings. Berridge (1997) points out that while this may be considered to be good practice, research by Rowe *et al* (1984) provides conflicting evidence; in general it is felt better to place siblings together where possible. However, it can be seen that where there are large family groups this can be difficult. While these children were in the residential home there was no contact made by the children's parents, Edward and Josephine. Given the relationship with their four other children, this may not be surprising. They may also have been deterred due to the practice of collecting fees from the parents in order to maintain the children.

Figures from the Home Office (1966) show that, during the financial year 1964-5, £1,046,634 was collected in parental contributions. This equated to over 6s (30p) per week for every child in care. While this would be an insignificant sum today, over 40 years ago it would have represented a significant cost, particularly where there were several children in care. It can be seen, therefore, how national policy could effectively discourage parental contact when there was a requirement to contribute financially towards the cost, particularly for those parents from lower socio-economic groups. Even if this contribution was not collected, the threat of being presented with a large bill may have been enough to deter some parents.

While Triseliotis (1989) argues that some foster parents were reluctant to accommodate biological parents and became increasingly hostile towards them, in the instance of these children, the reluctance to encourage contact from the biological parents was more based on fear. Having integrated the children into the family, Mr and Mrs Baker took on the role of substitute parents and developed a strong attachment to the children. While this may not have been an ideal situation, it should be remembered that at that time there was no training available for foster parents and very little by way of support networks. In 1978 Prosser commented:

> That foster parents might be offered some form of training for their job is, in this country, a comparatively recent idea and documentary evidence is slight.

> Where training schemes have been implemented they tend to be associated with special programmes to foster handicapped or disturbed children. (Prosser, 1978:34)

Although the children's biological parents did not attempt to make contact, there was always the fear of the children being removed from their care. Rowe *et al* (1984) suggest that for many of the children in long term foster care they would be better off adopted by their foster parents as this would provide the security which both parties crave. As suggested by Triseliotis and Hill (1987) these children came to look upon their foster carers as their parents, even calling them Mum and Dad. Sinclair *et al* (2005) highlight that particularly where children are fostered on a long term basis, there are still tensions today.

The long term outcomes for this family were largely positive. As mentioned previously, Mr and Mrs Baker, who had fostered Anne, Geraldine and Brian, asked for and obtained permission to adopt the children upon the death of their biological parents. All three of the children have gone on to have families of their own. Two have worked in some capacity with looked after children. The outcomes for the children who were looked after by the extended family also were largely positive. In his late teens, Peter took advantage of the £10 scheme and moved to Australia. Madeline and Elizabeth married and had families of their own. Madeline died relatively young aged 56. Jane lived with her grandmother until her grandmother died when she was about 16. She then went to live with the aunt who was also looking after Elizabeth. This arrangement broke down after a short period of time and she was placed with a specialist carer on a long term basis. The family are not in contact with Jane but it is believed she is currently being looked after within a specialist unit in the community. Most of the siblings have, within recent years, traced each other and are now in regular contact.

Between the mid 1960s and the late 1980s, as well as looking after their own three children (they had a further child in 1970), fostering the three members of the Wright family and another child on a long term basis, Mr and Mrs Baker fostered in excess of 60 further children on short, medium and long term basis. While the outcomes for the Wright family were largely positive, this was not the case for all of the children looked after by Mr and Mrs Baker. On at least two occasions Mr and Mrs Baker were advised that they would be caring for children on a long term and permanent basis, however, the child's biological parents' situation changed and the biological parents understandably wanted their child back. In both of these cases the father had remarried.

In one case the child was taken to live in the South of England to join his father, his father's new wife and her children from her previous marriage. Upon visiting the child a few months after he had moved, the foster parents found that the child had lost weight, was covered in bruises, was visibly withdrawn and appeared tired and dirty. After a short while the new relationship broke up and the child and his father moved back to the Midlands. Within a short while the child was taken back into local authority care. When Mr and Mrs Baker found out about this they asked to have the child returned to them but were advised that this was not possible. The other child had learning difficulties and his parents were unable to cope; again he returned to local authority care. While this is tragic for the children involved, it should also be remembered that this not only affects the foster parents but other children within the foster family who grieve for the loss of a sibling.

Current issues

This case raises a number of issues that are relevant today, as well as highlighting numerous areas in which significant changes have been made. As stated earlier, the 1963 Act made it a requirement for child care officers to consider prevention, yet in this case there appear only to have been limited attempts made by the Children's Department either to keep the family together or to support Edward and Josephine and to keep the family together. Although it has to be said that, given their learning difficulties, alcoholism and somewhat nomadic status this may have meant that the children might have been, at best, at significant risk of neglect, or at worst, of serious harm.

Cunningham (2006) highlights two opposing ideologies, the first believing that the family is the proper place for the child and that the state should not intervene, a view that prevailed in the 1980s and early 1990s. Social workers did in one much publicised case, however, remove children from their family homes on the suspicion that the children had been sexually abused, in this instance later proven not to be the case. The second view is that the State has an overriding duty to care for endangered children in the best interests of the child, even if this means removing parental rights.

At the time of writing, concerns have been raised by Lord Laming (Laming, 2009), whose report raises serious questions about the ability of some practitioners and local authorities to protect children from harm and neglect. The issue of whether or not to remove a child from their parental home is never one that is taken lightly, however. The Laming Report (2009) indicates that the training of some newly qualified practitioners leaves them ill equipped to undertake such decisions, with some practitioners never having had the opportunity to undertake training specifically relating to child protection issues; yet upon commencing their role they have a full caseload. This is acknowledged by the social workers themselves, with two-thirds of newly qualified social workers feeling that their academic training prepared them just enough, or not at all for their current role. It is therefore unsurprising that a recent report by the Audit Commission highlights that children's services are the least improved in a number of councils, and councils have had their performance ratings reduced as a consequence.

Points for discussion

- Consider the circumstances under which it might be necessary to remove children from their biological parents, bearing in mind the rights of the parents and of the children.

- Make a list of the types of training and support that might be important for foster parents to receive.

- Why is it important for children to retain contact with their biological families and what strategies might be effective in attempting to maintain this?

References

Berridge, D (1997) *Foster Care: a research review*. London: HMSO

Brandon, M, Belderson, P, Warren, C, Howe, D, Gardner, R, Dodsworth, J and Black, J (2008) *Analysing Child Deaths and Serious Injury through Abuse and Neglect: what can we learn? A biennial analysis of serious case reviews 2003-2005*. Nottingham: Department for Children Schools and Families

Chase, E, Simon, A and Jackson, S (eds) (2006) *In Care and After: a positive perspective*. Oxon: Routledge

Cunningham, H (2006) *The Invention of Childhood*. London: BBC Books

Curtis, M (1946) *Report of the Care of Children Committee*. Cmnd. 6922. London: HMSO

Department for Children, Schools and Families, (2008) *First Statistical Release Outcome Indicators for Children Looked After: Twelve Months to 30 September 2007*. England: DCSF

Hendrick, H (ed) (2005) *Child Welfare and Social Policy*. Bristol: The Policy Press

Home Office (1966) *Children in Care in England and Wales 1964/65*. London: HMSO

Home Office (1969) *Children in Care in England and Wales 1969*. London: HMSO

Laming, Lord W H (2009) *The Protection of Children in England: A progress report*. London: The Stationery Office

Prosser, H (1978) *Perspectives on Foster Care*. London: NFER

Rowe, J, Cain, H, Hundleby, M and Keane, A (1984) *Long-term Foster Care*. London: Batsford

Sinclair I, Baker, C, Wilson, K and Gibbs I (2005) *Foster Children: where they go and how they get on*. London: Kingsley Publishers

Taylor C (2006) Who will champion our vulnerable children? http://www.hm-treasury.gov.uk/d/cypreview2006_ssatrust2.pdf Accessed August 2009

Triseliotis, J (1989) Foster care outcomes: a review of key research findings. *Adoption and Fostering*, (13)3 p5-16

Triseliotis, J (2004) Foster care outcomes: a review of research findings. http:// www.scie-socialcareonline.org.uk/repository/fulltext/0003243.pdf Accessed January 2009

Triseliotis, J and Hill, M (1987) Children and adoption allowances. *Adoption and Fostering*. (11)1 p35-39

13

Integrated Care Strategies and Their Impact on Family Life in Glasgow: parents and children together

Eileen Carmichael

Introduction

Scotland, the northern part of the island of Britain, covers 78,722 square kilometres of land. Few parts of the country are more than 64 kilometres from the sea. Scotland has some 790 islands, few of which are inhabited. Its population in 2007 was estimated at 5,144,200 and there are concerns about a falling birth rate and an increasingly ageing population.

Glasgow is the largest city in Scotland and third most populous in the United Kingdom. The city is situated on the River Clyde in the country's west central lowlands. In the late nineteenth and twentieth centuries, Glasgow grew to a population of over one million, and was the fourth largest city in Europe, after London, Paris and Berlin. In the 1960s, large-scale relocation to new towns and peripheral suburbs, followed by successive boundary changes, has reduced the current population of the City of Glasgow to 580,690. The east end of the city has a population of around 90,000.

In the 1970s, the east end of Glasgow was a thriving community with high employment. It was reputed to be the area with the largest steel forge in the world, employing over 30,000 people, with many other associated employment opportunities. Today most industry has gone and the site of the forge is now a shopping mall. The area has become an industrial wasteland, with a community beset by chronic ill health, substance abuse, depression and unemployment. The east end of Glasgow has the highest proportion of Scotland's and Glasgow's most deprived areas with almost half the working age population unemployed and reliant upon state benefits.

The Scottish Government, concerned about the increasing number of children experiencing difficult family lives, has been looking at possible ways to promote child and family well-being for vulnerable and disadvantaged children. Glasgow now has two Parents and Children Together (PACT) teams based in each of its five Community Health and Care Partnership (CHCPs) areas. PACT is an integrated approach comprised of staff from health, social work and the voluntary sector with support from education services, and is able to involve other support agencies for specific support for families. PACT is funded and delivered as part of mainstream services within the CHCPs in Glasgow.

The aim of the approach is to ensure the provision of integrated packages of education, health and social work care for the most vulnerable and disadvantaged children and their families with a specific focus on good parenting.

The teams set out to:

- ensure the provision of integrated packages of education, health and social work care for the most vulnerable and disadvantaged children and their families
- complement the activities of generic services through ante-natal support, promoting effective child and family feeding and nutrition, promoting effective oral health and ensuring appropriate support for mothers experiencing post-natal mental health difficulties (including mothers from the ethnic minority communities)
- signpost and promote access by parents to appropriate health promotion initiatives and social care initiatives (Smoking Cessation, Safety Initiatives, Adult Education, Full Employment Initiatives etc)
- provide access for parents to a variety of individual and group-based models of parenting education opportunities within local areas
- ensure that families receive flexible childcare provision as required
- ensure that parents are consulted and involved in key decisions that affect them and their children
- reduce the vulnerability of low income families to financial exclusion and multiple debt (to prevent them becoming over-indebted and/or to lift them out of poverty)

Parents and Children Together (PACT) teams

Parents And Children Together teams are multi-agency, involving two health visitors, two social workers, two social care workers, two family support members, one nursery nurse and administrative support. Other advice workers, such as finance, dietetic or substance abuse advisers can also be involved to support a family. Family referral comes from health visitor, general practitioner or nursery head or by the social work service. The service in the east end of Glasgow started in 2005.

The approach involves partnership working with families, those who referred them and other services involved in supporting the family. The team aims to work in such a way as to enhance the inherent strengths of children and their parents, and promote positive change. This multi-disciplinary approach allows for a range of potential interventions to meet a variety of child and parental needs.

The PACT team approach is one of openness and honesty with families. To become involved with the team, the family must be prepared to look at their parenting and accept that they need support. It is clearly explained to families that their involvement with PACT will involve information being shared between agencies. For effective working with families it is crucial that they are willing to engage fully with PACT.

The PACT team approach can involve:

- individual work with parents and children to increase self esteem, promote play and development
- group work to look at children's development and or parental needs and
- practical support such as money advice, help in establishing household routines and access to other services.

Timescale
There is an agreed timescale of sixteen weeks from referral through acceptance then allocation of lead worker, development of initial action plan, including assessment, agreement about the intervention, interim review and final review. The final review may lead to handover to mainstream health or education services or the team may decide there is need for longer involvement with the family. A flow chart of the PACT care pathway can be found on http://www.healthscotland.com/uploads/documents/Care%20pathway%20flow%20chart%2021.06.06.doc Accessed August 2009.

There are many success stories in which the PACT teams have helped families turn their lives around. This Chapter will concentrate on two families.

Kenneth and Jane and their family

Kenneth and Jane have four children, three girls (aged 5, 4 and 3) fathered by Jane's previous partner and a son (aged one year), fathered by Kenneth. The children had been referred to the Children's Panel as in need of care and protection and likely to be in need of being accommodated away from their home.

In Scotland, in 1971, children's hearings took over from the courts most of the responsibility for dealing with children and young people under 16, and in some cases under 18, who commit offences or who are in need of care and protection. The hearing discusses the circumstances of the child fully with the parents, the child or young person and any representatives, the social worker and the teacher, if present. As the hearing is concerned with the wider picture and the long term well-being of the child, the measures on which it decides will be based on the welfare of the child. This system is unique to Scotland.

Information on Scotland's distinctive system of care and justice for its children and young people can be found on http://www.childrens-hearings. co.uk/ and http://www.chscotland.gov.uk/background.asp Accessed August 2009.

It was decided at a child protection case conference, as part of the child protection care plan, to place the children's names on the Child Protection Register and involve the family with the local PACT team.

The family live in a four roomed flat on the top floor of a three storey building. Jane said:'It's the worst street' (and the Social Work Department confirms massive social work involvement in homes in the street). 'You cannot let them out to play – there's drugs and dogs' urine everywhere.'

When the PACT lead worker visited the house, she found that the children's general hygiene was very poor and they were heavily infested with head lice. The house was chaotic: dirty and smelly, with food and household belongings lying everywhere. It was thought that the children had been used to finding food for themselves, climbing up onto work surfaces There were few toys or books and the lack of supervision of the children led to serious concerns about their safety. Jane had very low self-esteem and to quote the lead worker it was, 'very difficult to engage with both parents', who felt 'Sick of too many people coming in and out of the house. It's as if they don't trust you with your own children. '

The PACT action plan was for intensive family support. The lead worker visited the house daily, provided equipment such as safety gates, and acted as a role model to help establish routines for the children and in caring for the home, acquired funds to buy storage for the household items strewn around the house. (The girls' father, Jane's past partner, had smashed up the house and been violent to Jane in front of the children.) There was help with budgeting, supervised food shopping trips and basic cooking. A nursery nurse visited the family three times a week for five weeks, showing the parents how to identify and treat their own and the children's head lice. Toys were bought for the children who had had little to play with at home.

Nursery places were allocated to the three youngest children and the eldest, a 5-year-old in primary school, started to attend an after-school homework club one day a week. The Health Visitor made regular visits and team members liaised regularly with the nursery and primary school.

While the children were in school and nursery, there was time for the team to work with Kenneth and Jane. The lead worker accompanied Jane to a women's art therapy group. Jane was at first reluctant to become involved with the group but persevered in order to keep her children at home. Attempts to involve her with a literacy support group, because of low literacy skills, did not succeed. Jane has said she 'did not like it, it was not much use.'

Kenneth, who had a prison record and low self-esteem and literacy skills, was supported to address his drug use through changing to a methadone programme and to begin to think about looking for employment.

Together Jane and Kenneth attended weekly parenting groups looking at their family needs and finding out about child development, including how to interact and play with their children. Kenneth came to realise that sending the children to bed at perhaps 4 pm because of boisterous play, was not the best way to manage their behaviour. He was initially content to sit and watch TV leaving Jane to cope with both children and cook the meal, until the lead worker made it clear to him that he could provide more support to Jane by playing with the children while she made meals. It was agreed there would be limited time when the television would be switched on in the evenings, and regular family outings to the local park and other local amenities were arranged.

It was not easy for Jane and Kenneth but they were aware that, by not co-operating, the children were likely to be taken into care. Jane said she felt they were 'going forward and slipping back' but the extensive and continual external support of the PACT team, the nursery and the school was in time much appreciated. The lead worker, by helping them to develop routines for both children and home (which was a significant part of her role), came to be trusted and regarded positively. Over time, Kenneth and Jane began to realise that their family life was much improved and becoming enjoyable.

The children, who had been very quiet and withdrawn at school and nursery, began to blossom. There were no longer concerns about their cleanliness. The eldest girl had had to be given urgent dental treatment because of her early diet. A dietician was brought in to work with the family, and the younger children exhibit no dental decay. As their parents were helped with shopping for food and preparing healthy meals the children grew and flourished. Self esteem grew for all of them. 'Now my mum says she loves me', says the eldest girl.

The younger children grew happy and confident in nursery. Both parents are keen to chat with nursery and school staff, talking about their plans for later in the day. Both parents responded to the school and nursery unobtrusively being there for them, showing interest in them and building their confidence. The girls' paternal grandmother was also very supportive, keeping contact with the family and often having all four children to stay with her at week-ends.

Kenneth is working part-time now as a security guard and, if he remains drug-free, there is the possibility of work experience in the local area in preparation for the 2014 Commonwealth Games. Once the children are older, Jane plans to study to be a hairdresser.

This intensive daily support continued for some five months. Gradually evening and weekend monitoring of the family stopped. Over many months the PACT team involvement lessened. The family social worker had worked very hard to gain their trust and succeeded. His regular visits continued and, two years after the children's names were added to the child protection register, their names were removed. All agencies, social work, health and education, agreed the children were no longer at risk. Jane recently said about the family social worker:

> They're made out to be bad people who take your children away but he really helped us. Things now could not be any better.

Kenneth says, 'I am so happy now, ' and their social worker believes that, 'Now they are a family, a happy family. '

Margaret, Brian and Keir

Keir was born very prematurely and addicted to the drugs his mother had been using. He has a chronic lung condition and some learning difficulties. At the time of his birth, he was placed on the Child Protection Register and the maternal grandmother, who has multiple sclerosis, agreed to care for Keir on a voluntary basis prior to him living with her, as a condition of a supervision requirement. He remained in hospital for some three months after his birth. At this time, Margaret, his mother, was placed on a methadone programme to wean her off drugs. She did express guilt that her lifestyle was the cause of Keir's difficulties. She was in her early twenties, possibly involved in prostitution, and known to be closely connected to other drug users. Brian, the father, who was some ten years older than Margaret, became drug free while serving a prison sentence for assault after Keir's birth.

The couple lived together when Brian came out of prison but then split up. Margaret went back to stay with her mother before being allocated her own home. Brian helped her to decorate it and always kept contact with Keir. He attended the regular child protection case conferences with Margaret. The grandmother was initially very hostile to Brian, blaming him for her daughter's plight and worried that she would lose custody of Keir to him.

The family health visitor referred Keir and the family to the PACT team because of the need for support to attend medical appointments for Keir, now aged 2, and for Margaret regarding parenting issues. Margaret was still involved in drug abuse. Following referral, the lead worker visited Margaret and Keir at home, a flat on the 28th floor of a tower block. Keir looked well cared for, as did the home. Margaret was evasive with the lead worker but did agree to work with the PACT team.

Keir was given a nursery place where he was very highly active and found it difficult to relate to the other children. Over time he became much calmer and is now popular with the other children. The nursery staff report that Keir's behaviour has greatly improved as a result of the team's work with the family. His health condition is always likely to be a problem and some learning difficulties remain.

Margaret agreed to work with a support worker from the addiction team. At that time she was 'small, gaunt, with dead hair and not very outgoing'. Now she has filled out and looks healthy. She attended an art therapy course in the nursery, funded by Glasgow City Council. Now she is organised and responsible. PACT is supporting her in a work preparation programme and she hopes to go on to further study at college.

Brian also became involved with the team who facilitated his contact with Keir, supporting him in his relationship with Keir and helping him to learn about children's development. Brian went on to complete a social care course at college. Nursery staff suggested to him that he consider employment in childcare. He is keen to discuss Keir's work with nursery staff daily and to talk about his plans for Keir later that day, perhaps some baking or a park visit.

The lead worker organised transport for Keir to the nursery and for Margaret to enable her to attend the appointments with other support agencies. She also had to negotiate with the hospital to resume Keir's check ups as he had been removed from the lists because so many past appointments had been missed. Appointments were restarted. Brian and Margaret attended each one together.

While Margaret and Brian are very unlikely ever to live together again as a couple, they now see a positive future ahead for themselves and they are, 'both very committed parents who love Keir to bits'. Keir's grandmother remains highly supportive of her daughter and Keir and now she speaks very positively about Brian. There is currently very light, and reducing, social work involvement with the family.

Keeping families together

These are only two examples of the interagency support and collaboration being developed in and by the PACT teams across Glasgow. There could have been many more such examples. It is intensive and expensive; perhaps, however, it is money well spent as shown in these two examples. The parents have been supported to become 'a proper and happy family' compared with the financial and emotional cost of taking Kenneth and Jane's four children into care for (perhaps) many years, and the cost of a difficult start for Keir with parents who had few positive future prospects and ambitions.

In this project there is trust among the staff from different agencies. They work together for families, supporting each other. The nursery is supportive and welcoming to parents. Staff are sensitive to parental needs and work to boost their self esteem. The PACT team leader says the nursery, despite having a high number of very vulnerable children with the full range of difficulties seen in the local area, offers respite and opportunities for children – play and learning, socialisation and routines. This provides time for the PACT team to work with the parents. The nursery will offer flexible childcare to allow parents to attend parenting classes in the nursery or late afternoon classes in another local venue. There is excellent multi-agency communication and teamwork.

The city of Glasgow, Scotland, has been chosen to host the 2014 Commonwealth Games. Sports facilities and the athletes' village, leaving a new housing legacy, will be developed in the area. There is a sense of hope that change is coming to the area and will be long lasting.

Role and function of multi-agency working

In recent years there has been much research about multi-agency working in a number of areas.

In *Multi-agency working and its implications for practice: a review of the literature,* Atkinson *et al* (2007) review findings about different models, impact, influencing factors and effective practice. Appendix 5 p99, lists the definition of terms relating to multi-agency activity used in the research review.

Lessons in Change: a journey towards delivering integrated services for children, (NHS Health Scotland, 2008), is research specifically about the PACT development. It outlines the development of the approach across Glasgow and indicates reasons for success and possible future pitfalls.

In Scotland, the *Early Years Framework* (Scottish Executive, 2009) aims to develop a simpler, integrated structure of services to support families. It draws on research and sets out the short, medium and long term aims in developing this support.

A Practitioner's Guide to Interagency Working in Children's Centres: a review of literature (McInnes, K, 2007) looks specifically at the views of some practitioners in children's centres and contains this quote from a practitioner:

> Interagency working is about making sure that people are regularly talking about their work, understanding each others' roles and sharing with other agencies and service users. It is about working together towards commonly agreed aims and objectives (No page, website).

Points for discussion

- ■ What range of professionals is required to support families such as those described in this Chapter and what is the role of each?
- ■ Outline the considerations required for successful team working.

References

Atkinson, M, Jones, M and Lamont, E (2007) *Multi-agency Working and Its Implications for Practice: a review of the literature.* Reading: CfBT http://www.cfbt.com/evidenceforeducation/pdf/New%20in%20template%202.pdf Accessed August 2009

McInnes, K (2007) A Practitioner's Guide to Inter-agency Working in Children's Centres: a review of literature. Barnardo's online http://www.barnardos.org.uk/a_practitioner_s_guide_to_interagency_working_-_final_report_-_april_2007.pdf Accessed August 2009

NHS Health Scotland (2006) PACT Pathway Flow Chart. http://www.healthscotland.com/uploads/documents/Care%20pathway%20flow%20chart%2021.06.06.doc Accessed August 2009

NHS Health Scotland (2008) Lessons in Change: a journey towards delivering integrated services for children http://www.healthscotland.com/documents/2916.aspx Accessed August 2009

Scottish Executive, 2009 Early Years Framework. http://www.scotland.gov.uk/Publications/2009/01/13095148/0 Accessed August 2009

Further websites

Scottish Executive (web only 2008) A Guide to Getting it Right for Every Child. http://www.scotland.gov.uk/Publications/2008/09/22091734/0 Accessed August 2009

Glasgow City Council Protecting Children: information for service providers. http://www.glasgow.gov.uk/NR/rdonlyres/783BC275-EEB0-4635-824B-A087C5A6E1BD/0/GlasgowChildProtectionProtectingChildren.pdf Accessed August 2009

Scottish Executive Children's Hearings http://www.childrens-hearings.co.uk/ Accessed August 2009 http://www.chscotland.gov.uk/background.asp Accessed August 2009

Sincere thanks to the staff of Glasgow City Council who gave me the inspiration and information for the case study

Section V
Challenges and Changes

Two very different topics are addressed in Chapters 14 and 15, which are both relevant to children growing up in the twenty-first century. Adults vary greatly in their views about the value of introducing children to digital technology at an early age. Many view it as a negative influence on children's creativity, but is it and need it be? Chapter 14 presents insights from a research project in Scotland into the knowledge of and competence in digital technology of young children based on their experience in their home before starting school. Although the Rights of the Child is highlighted in many current documents, many adults still believe young children to lack the competence to be actively involved in planning their own activities. Chapter 15 describes the extent to which young children in a family in Copenhagen are enabled to be involved in decision making at home, in school and in the wider community. These examples challenge the many adults who assume that young children lack competence and give them few opportunities to have a real voice in shaping their environment.

In the final Chapter (16) we guide readers in looking again at the life stories of the young children described in this book, grouping the issues under rather different headings. There are many early childhoods, and the stories told here show the challenges faced by young children and their families, the resilience of many, and the as yet unfulfilled needs of others.

- Make a list of the range of technologies you would expect young children to have experienced before they start school
- What influence would you expect social class to have on this? You may have some surprises when you study this research
- In what ways do you think young children could be given a voice in decision making in the home and in school?
- In the light of what you have read in this book, consider whether the term 'the global child' is a useful concept

14

Digital Technologies at Home: the experiences of 3- and 4-year-olds in Scotland

Christine Stephen, Joanna McPake
and Lydia Plowman

Introduction: digital technology: blessing or curse?

This Chapter is about young children's experiences with digital technologies that are a now familiar part of their home life. In a survey of 346 families conducted in Scotland by the authors in 2005, we found that most children aged 3 and 4 years were growing up in homes where a range of digital technologies was in use (Plowman *et al*, 2008a). Regardless of income levels, most of our survey respondents' children were living in households where there was access to a mobile phone (98%), interactive TV (75%) and a computer with internet access (69%). Two-thirds (64%) of the children living in homes with an Internet connection made use of it for looking at websites, typically with adult supervision, although ten per cent used websites on their own. About half the children (48%) used a mobile phone with adult help.

The advent of digital technologies has been heralded on the one hand as offering great potential for young children and on the other as a threat to their natural development or as another source of division and disadvantage. There is a debate between those who advocate the use of technology as a way of facilitating or enhancing learning and others who are concerned that using new technology is harmful for preschool children and who argue for the value of traditional toys. Those who argue that children need to be confident and competent users of new technologies claim that children will flourish and be prepared for the future through their interactions with computers, video games and hand-held games consoles (eg Prensky, 2006; Shaffer, 2007). On the other side of the argument, there are claims that new technologies can take over children's time for play, distracting them from other more active and positive traditional pursuits and threatening their cognitive, social and emotional development (eg Cordes and Miller, 2000; Palmer, 2006).

The policy environment in Scotland is supportive of children's use of digital technologies in preschool settings and at home. In 2003 the Scottish Executive launched a strategy aimed at developing the use of information and communication technologies (ICT) in preschool settings in the public, private and voluntary sectors. The policy was concerned with developing appropriate pedagogical practices, ensuring equal access for all children, encouraging providers to obtain resources and offering training for practitioners. We found positive attitudes towards new technologies amongst the parents we interviewed. When prompted by attitude statements, they were ready to discuss some of the claims about the negative impact of children's interactions with technology, eg that inactivity contributes to obesity, or that computer games are addictive. Nevertheless, each family felt that they had achieved a balance between time spent with technology and time with more traditional activities and all were keen to ensure that their children had a broad range of everyday activities and experiences (Plowman *et al*, 2008a). Their 3- to 5-year-olds had opportunities to use a wide range of technologies at home: digital cameras, Wii, remote controlled cars, interactive television, games consoles, internet computer games and resources aimed specifically at young children, eg the V-tech range of interactive toys. However, these parents reported that their children frequently played in the garden or went to the play park, played with dolls and cars, rode bicycles, used slides and swings and went swimming and to the soft play room. (Plowman *et al*, 2008b).

Exploring preschool children using technology at home

In this Chapter we draw on findings from *Entering e-Society*, one of a series of Economic and Social Research Council-funded studies which we have completed, exploring young children's encounters with new technology. In *Entering e-Society* we focused on the experiences that 3- and 4-year-olds have with new technologies in their own homes. Through case studies of nineteen families over a period of one year we built rich portraits of the children's lives. We explored the perspectives of their parents towards new technologies, the influence of parents' own early experiences with ICT, parental expectations about the place of technology in the children's futures and the ways in which parents try to support children as they use the technological resources available at home. We also took care to ensure that we captured the perspectives of the 3- and 4-year-olds, without which our understanding of young children's use of digital technologies at home would have been incomplete. Through the methods which we developed to explore the perspectives of young learners, we found that they are active and discriminating users of technology with decided preferences and a view of their own competencies (Stephen *et al*, 2008)

The case study families participating in *Entering e-Society* lived in central Scotland, in or near to urban areas of varying size and economic status. Their socio-economic circumstances varied from comfortable and advantaged to disadvantaged and living on government benefits. In some cases, both parents held jobs with good salaries, the family owned their home and two cars and could afford holidays abroad. In other cases, mothers were bringing up their children alone in public sector housing, with or without the support of their extended family and with little money left after basic needs were covered. Among the group of 24 children whose parents volunteered at the beginning of the case study phase, there were eleven girls and thirteen boys: seventeen lived in two-parent families and seven in one-parent families. Thirteen were from households with an income greater than £20,000 per annum and eleven from homes where the income was less than £15,000 per annum.

All of the case study children attended a preschool education setting, either for the five half-day sessions each week funded by the government for every 3- and 4-year-old, or for more extended hours while their parents worked. By the time they were ready to start school, most of the children had experience of using and watching others use a broad range of technologies in their own homes and those of friends and relatives, including telephones, computers, electronic musical instruments, MP3, CD and cassette players, televisions, video and DVD players, still and video cameras, games consoles and domestic appliances. Many had toy laptops or digital games bought to support literacy and numeracy and interactive, electronic books.

Creating a digital divide?

There is a widespread concern that the development of digital technology has created another divide between children from different economic backgrounds. However, our data suggest that there is no simple divide between the experiences of economically advantaged and disadvantaged children. For example, in our survey we found that among those who did not have access to the internet at home 29 per cent had an income of less than £8,500 while 30 per cent had an income of more than £20,000. We found a complex relationship between family circumstances and ICT experiences, one that is the result of family practices, parental attitudes and children's own preferences.

In some economically advantaged families, parents did not prioritise competency with new technology and were happy to wait until their child expressed an interest or when they started school. On the other hand, some families with lower income gave priority to acquiring a computer because they thought this was important for their children's futures. Families with lower income but a positive attitude towards their child engaging with new technology made the most of the resources they had (typically a TV and mobile phone). For instance, Kirsty's mum was a single parent who did not work but she was an able computer user and keen to ensure that her daughter could use digital technologies. Kirsty was able to use the TV controls independently, was an enthusiastic user of her LeapPad, an interactive book console, and accessed children's websites on her grandmother's computer.

A more powerful influence on parental attitudes and behaviour towards technology was the adults' own experience of technology and its value for the kinds of things they did at work (eg managing databases or architectural design), at home (eg online banking or shopping) and for leisure and entertainment (eg using a playstation or watching videos). The examples of Grace and Catriona (Box 1) illustrate the influence of their parents' engagement with ICT and their perspective on the value of young children using new technologies. Both girls lived in economically advantaged families and their parents had all had experience of using ICT at school and for work. However, while Catriona had become a competent user of the technology at home, Grace had few technological toys, preferred traditional activities and had little interest in technologies. The experiences and technological competencies of the girls are related to the attitudes of their parents. Grace's mother in particular sees little or no need for her daughter to use technology at present as she argues that early knowledge and skills will become obsolete and she is concerned about the impact of computer games on the behaviour of children and adults. On the other hand, using ICT is very much a part of the everyday life of Catriona's mother and is becoming a very familiar feature of her daughter's experience, too.

Box 1 Grace and Catriona: the impact of parental attitudes

Grace and Catriona were two 4-year-old girls from families defined by us as advantaged. Both had 6-year-old brothers and their parents had similar backgrounds. Their fathers had skilled jobs requiring specialist technical competences. Grace's mother was a childminder and Catriona's was involved in home care for the elderly. Grace's parents had early experiences of learning to use ICT. Her father had gained a qualification in computing at school while her mother had learned basic programming and the use of accountancy software packages to help with her parents' business. Catriona's mother had gained an HNC qualification in computing immediately after leaving school and had worked as an ICT trainer in the National Health Service. Her father used specialist technologies associated with his work as a marine pilot and more recently had become a competent user of the home computer.

However, the attitudes of the two sets of parents towards children's use of new technologies were very different. Grace's parents had negative views of their early experiences with ICT, describing these as boring and irrelevant, and now very out of date. Grace's mother was concerned that video games make children aggressive and that having internet access at home would encourage her husband to become 'addicted to the internet'. She believed that any technological skills acquired now will quickly become obsolete and that there was therefore no urgency about children learning to use ICT. In contrast, Catriona's parents were confident and enthusiastic users of home technologies, using the internet for shopping and banking. 'How did I ever manage without it?' Catriona's mother asked, They had positive views of technology in the future, and believed that children should take every opportunity to develop the technological skills which would enable them to take advantage of developments.

Grace's and Catriona's own abilities to use new technologies appeared to be related to their parents' attitudes and experiences. Grace had very limited skills. Unusually among our case-study children, she could not use the TV controls, and had virtually no technically oriented items, other than a toy Barbie CD player and a toy Barbie laptop. Her favourite activities are playing with Barbie dolls, dressing up, playing outdoors and swimming. At the same age, Catriona was fully competent with TV controls and with a mobile phone. She played computer games with her older brother although she needed some help with setting games up. Her favourite activities included playing with dolls, painting, in the traditional way or on the computer, watching TV and playing computer games. By the end of our visits, Catriona could find favourite websites on the internet, enjoyed the Dancemat, had decreed LeapPads and VTech toys to be too babyish for her, and could take pictures with the digital camera, though she had not learned to review or download them onto the computer yet. Her mother was pleased that she was 'not frightened' of ICT.

Children's preferences

In addition to the influence that their families have on children's engagement with technology, the children's own individual preferences and enduring interests and dispositions play an important part in shaping their use of ICT. Children who were cautious and keen to avoid failure were reported by their parents to take a similar approach to using digital technologies. Others were described as explorers who confidently launched into new games or puzzled over and mastered new devices. If a child had an enduring interest, for example in sport like Alexander, or cars and trucks like Kenneth, this was often reflected in the ways in which they engaged with technology. Alexander particularly enjoyed computer games on a sports website while Kenneth liked to take digital photographs of vehicles and to use his remote controlled cars.

The children themselves made it clear that they had distinct preferences among traditional toys and activities and technological resources and there was no evidence that using ICT in leisure and family time dominated the children's choices. All of the children involved in *Entering e-Society* identified traditional activities among the things that they were good at and enjoyed doing. About half of them identified playing on a slide and swimming as activities they enjoyed. Drawing was also a popular choice. Over two-thirds said that playing with the computer made them happy and about half were happy to watch television. The children stopped using a technological resource if it became boring or too hard to be an attractive activity. For instance, Angus did not like the alphabet game because he said it was too hard, and Grace complained about having difficulty making the cursor move on some games. Andy thought that playing with his Gameboy was sometimes boring. The children used technology when it was fun or enjoyable and did not see it as a learning activity or work in the way they often describe adult-initiated activities in school.

In their accounts of using new technologies, and their descriptions about how other children the same age could learn to use the resources, the case study children were able to differentiate between operational competence (knowing how to use the technology) and being able to complete the tasks, games or activities that the technology permitted.

> Using the controller [for the Playstation] can be hard because there are so many buttons it's hard to use them all at once. (Kenneth)

> [It's hard] because you've got to try to use the white one to get the balloons to burst them ... you've got to catch them. (Grace, referring to Disney Plug 'N' Play)

Not only did the children have decided preferences, they were also able to evaluate their own competencies, indicating which technologies they were good at using and those with which they struggled. Catriona told the researchers that she was good at the Bob the Builder computer game. Freddie said that he was good at the Pokemon computer game but failed with a Toy Story game: 'I die on that one, it's rubbish, too hard'.

The children most frequently nominated their parents as a source of help with technology and parents clearly provided opportunities for the children, supported their emergent skills and interests and purchased equipment that they thought would give their children pleasure. Nevertheless, although their parents and siblings could provide a context that encouraged the use of particular resources, perhaps using the webcam or downloading and listening to music, the 3- and 4-year-olds resisted playing with technology which they did not find attractive or which did not fit with their interests. Stuart (Box 2) was growing up in a household with ample technological resources and his family are keen users of ICT. However, the presence of technology at home (and in his nursery) did not drive Stuart's interests. He chose not to engage in these activities but followed his own interests in outdoor and physical play.

Box 2 Stuart: no interest in digital technologies

Four-year-old Stuart was described by his mother as a very active boy who loved the outdoors, cycling and playing action games. He had little interest in computers or playing electronic games or even watching TV or DVDs. The family lived in a technology-rich home and both parents made use of ICT in their work and for leisure and household activities. Chris, Stuart's 6-year-old brother, had developed an early interest in new technologies. By the time he was 3-years-old Chris was able to use the TV and DVD player and was now quickly picking up the skills he needed, such as Internet surfing. In contrast, Stuart remained fundamentally uninterested in using digital technologies. At the age of 5 years, he finally learned to use the TV and DVD remote controls by himself, but had little interest in or ability to use the computer, or the X-box.

Learning with technology

In our earlier study of children learning with ICT in preschool settings (Stephen and Plowman, 2008), we identified three kinds of learning:

- operational learning (how to use the technology)
- learning about areas of the curriculum through using technology (eg about animals or cities, identifying rhymes, sorting and categorising)

■ acquiring positive learning dispositions such as confidence and persistence.

The children learned as they used technology at home, too. Here, the key areas of learning were operational, social and cultural. They developed operational skills, such as learning how to switch on and off, select channels or use icons, rewind or record and how to store and retrieve data. They learned, too, about the social uses of the technologies as they joined their families in communicating with friends and relatives by talking or sending texts on mobile phones, using webcams or sending photographs by email. Cultural learning opportunities came through engaging with a wide range of activities facilitated by digital technologies, ranging from watching and interacting with television or DVDs, playing games or creating scenarios on websites to creating pictures or photographs and video clips.

Digital literacy can be defined as being able to understand and employ a range of technological sources to develop knowledge and potential and achieve goals. In these terms, the children in our study were developing digital literacy likely to be important for future success. Print literacy and digital literacy seem to be mutually enhancing as they offer children experience of alternative forms of symbolic representation (words, numbers, icons). Print, sound and visual representations are increasingly integrated in the multi-media world of digital technology and this offers opportunities to develop interlinked competencies and complementary forms of expression (Yelland *et al*, 2008).

At home, learning was driven by participating in authentic, shared activities that allowed the child to become a participant in the practices of the family and community. Parents and other family members did sometimes give direct instructions to their 3- or 4-year-olds about how to use equipment but more often they talked of how the children just 'picked it up' as they participated in everyday family practices (Plowman *et al*, 2008b). This contrasted with their experiences in preschool settings where the children seldom saw practitioners using technology to communicate or acquire information and were much less likely to be involved in using the technology to achieve personal goals (Stephen and Plowman, 2008; Plowman and Stephen, 2007). In addition, at home the range of resources is likely to be richer and more frequently available to any individual child than at nursery or playgroup where some resources such as computers are sometimes old or handed down and children may have to share one digital camera with fifteen or twenty others.

In educational settings, particularly when children move on to primary school, the focus tends to be on learning how to use resources or on completing activities in carefully prescribed ways which can fail to take account of the social and cultural learning and skills developed at home and children's individual preferences and strengths. In our study, none of the parents with a child moving to school reported being asked how their child used technologies at home, indeed, one mother told us that her child's teacher said that at school children would be taught how to use the keyboard and mouse 'properly', This approach risks failing to build on the operational, problem solving and creative competencies children have developed as they use digital technologies at home and does not maximise the potential of their existing funds of knowledge (Gonzalez *et al*, 2005)

In conclusion

In this Chapter we have described how preschool children engage with new technologies at home. The concern that technology is opening another divide between children from different socio-economic backgrounds is not supported by our evidence. Our findings suggest that parents' own encounters with and expectations of ICT, and their family values and practices, are likely to have a stronger influence than economic factors on the experiences that children have with technologies at home. Parents do have some anxieties about exposing children to the negative influences associated with technology, such as physical inactivity, or the endorsement of aggressive behaviour. However, most families were confident that they were achieving an appropriate balance of traditional or technological play, entertainment and risk or opportunity. They took steps to regulate encounters with technology if they felt it was necessary (eg limiting the length of time watching DVDs or playing computer games).

The children themselves were active and influential agents in the activities they undertook at home. All of the children in our study selected traditional activities amongst the things that they preferred to do and felt they were good at, and there was no evidence that using technologies dominated their play. As they participated in family life, the children were able to learn how to operate technologies and they experienced what could be achieved with particular resources. However, they did not necessarily choose to engage with technology even if their parents and siblings were enthusiastic users. The children were discriminating users of technologies who had decided preferences, were ready to stop if the activity was too difficult or not interesting enough, and were able to evaluate their own performances. Through their interactions with technologies at home, the 3- and 4-year-olds were developing digital literacy and acquiring operational social and cultural competencies. If this learning is to be built on in preschool and primary school, it is important for preschool practitioners and teachers to be aware of the rich and varied ways in which children use digital technologies at home and the skills and understandings which they bring to school as a result of these encounters with ICT.

Points for discussion

■ What are the arguments for and against young children using digital technologies?

■ How are digital technologies changing the ways that children and their parents learn?

■ What questions should practitioners ask parents about children using digital technologies at home so that learning in preschool and primary school can build on learning at home?

References

Cordes, C and Miller, E (eds) (2000) *Fool's Gold: a critical look at computers in childhood.* College Park, MD: Alliance for Childhood

Gonzalez, N, Moll, L and Amanti, C (eds) (2005) *Funds of knowledge: theorizing practices in households, communities and classrooms.* Mahwah, NJ: Erlbaum

Palmer, S (2006) *Toxic Childhood: how the modern world is damaging our children and what we can do about it.* London: Orion

Plowman, L, McPake, J and Stephen, C (2008a) The technologisation of childhood? Young children and technology in the home. Children and Society, published online August 2008. Available at http://www3.interscience.wiley.com/cgi-bin/fulltext/121385522/PDFSTART Accessed May 2009

Plowman L, McPake, J and Stephen, C (2008b) Just picking it up? Young children learning with technology at home, *Cambridge Journal of Education,* 38(3) p303-319

Plowman, L and Stephen, C (2007) Guided interaction in pre-school settings. *Journal of Computer Assisted Learning,* 23(1) p14-21

Prensky, M (2006) *Don't Bother Me Mom – I'm Learning!* St Paul, Minnesota: Paragon House

Shaffer, D (2007) *How Computer Games Help Children Learn,* New York: Palgrave Macmillan

Stephen, C, McPake, J, Plowman, L and Berch-Heyman, S (2008) Learning from the children: exploring preschool children's encounters with ICT at home. *Journal of Early Childhood Research,* 6(2) p99-117

Stephen, C and Plowman, L (2008) Enhancing learning with information and communication technologies in pre-school. *Early Child Development and Care,* 178(6) p637-654

Yelland, N, Lee, L, O'Rourke, M and Harrison, C (2008) *Rethinking Learning in Early Childhood Education.* Maidenhead: Open University Press

15

A Voice in Decision Making: young children in Denmark

Stig Broström

Introduction

This Chapter focuses on the life of young children. It views the child as an active and valid member of society, a democratic, communicating and participating person. The child is seen as a competent person, able to take part in and influence his or her daily life. Theoretical and practical examples are given, and the Chapter explores not only how to bring up children as active democrats, but also how to encourage them to make use of their competences from an early age in order to contribute to society. The reader is encouraged to reflect on possibilities and problems surrounding the idea of young children's participation and influence on society.

Society and democracy

In Western societies attempts are frequently made to understand the principle of democracy from one overall perspective. The German scholar Jürgen Habermas (1994) argues that to take capitalism at its own word, and to strive for a real democratic society, there are four rules for non-controlling communication; a communication in which understanding, truth, correctness and honesty are expressed.

From a social point of view like this, educational strategies aim at *Bildung* and democracy. The German concept *Bildung* (Klafki, 1998) offers an alternative or contrasting perspective to traditional ideas of socialisation. Instead of being socialised into the social system, accepting the rules of society without critical reflection, Bildung supports people in reflecting on the preconditions for what occurs around them and with them; it emancipates humans to be political subjects. This ambitious idea aims to make the world transparent for children. Thus, a Bildung based approach listens to children's perspectives and gives them the possibility to influence their daily lives. Using the words of the American scholar Giroux, Bildung should

> not only empower students by giving them the knowledge and skills they need to be able to function in the larger society as critical agents, but also educate them for the transformative action in the interest of creating a truly democratic society. (Giroux, 1988:xxxiii)

Children are seen as active, competent subjects and thus the teacher supports the individual child's initiatives, interests and perspectives. James *et al*, (1998) argue that societal changes during the last two or three decades have paved the way for the emergence of a new type of childhood, characterised first of all by individualisation, often extended to include children's responsibility for their own learning. This results in a more extensive democratic education and everyday life.

Early childhood legislation

Not only in Denmark but in all the Nordic countries, the democratic dimension is mentioned in the aims for children's learning and development in preschool. In Denmark, the *Daginstitutiosloven* (2007) demands that day care centres must contribute to and support children's understanding of democracy and integration into Danish society (Daginstitutionsloven, 2007).

The act emphasises children's right to be taken seriously and protected. Though children do not have their own official ombudsman, Denmark has established a *Børneråd*, children's advisory board, which ensures that children's voices are not only heard, but also correctly understood within the larger society.

Most important for the protection and promotion of children was the creation of the *United Nations Convention of the Rights of the Child* (1989). This landmark legislation delineated rights for children and expressed a vision and a hope for children the world over. Related to the theme of valuing children's perspectives, the Convention specifies four fundamental and universal rights for children:

> the right to survive
> the right to develop to the fullest

the right to protection from harmful influences, abuse and exploitation; and
the right to participate fully in family, cultural and social life

This legal foundation gives the opportunity for educators to create a theoretical and practical approach in promoting children's influence and active participation in society.

Theoretical background for the communicating and participating child

Numerous childhood sociologists have described changes in various aspects of childhood's structure and content. They look at childhood as a social construction and argue for the study of childhood, children's relations, and children's culture in their own right, rather than as a consequence of external social forces and influences (Brannen and O'Brien, 1995; James *et al*, 1998). Proponents of this perspective see children as whole and complete persons with their own status, needs and rights, and not as incomplete versions of the adults they will become. Thus children are not seen as incompetent human beings who have to go through a primary socialisation to establish a fundamental trust or secure attachment before they can meet the outer world with new peers and adults. They are competent and ready to participate in social life, even as newborns (see for example, Trevarthen, 1998).

The importance of children's views and voices has become a central theme in recent childhood education and forms the basis of the phrase the communicating and participating child.

The child as active participant

Embedded in the above understanding, children are seen as social agents, in other words as active participants in their own development and important contributors to society (Jensen and Schnack, 1997). Modern perspectives on childhood, coupled with a growing faith in children's competence, and views of children as human beings rather than human becomings create potential pathways for children to participate in society. Where children are seen as competent and contributing members of a democratic society and as having rights – in other words as active participants – teachers, politicians and parents are more willing to consider a child perspective. However, with reference to Qvarsell (2003), when educators and researchers talk about a child perspective, they may refer to one or other of two different orientations:

(a) they may focus their attention on the ways in which adults look at children and reflect on what they, as adults, perceive to be the children's perspectives, or

(b) they may focus on how children look at their own world, their conditions and themselves (adapted from Qvarsell, 2003).

Thus, the concept child perspective encompasses how adults and society try to understand children's lives, as well as how children themselves experience and describe their lives.

Throughout the 1990s researchers have attempted to capture the essential multi-sidedness of the concept. For example, the Finnish researcher Kerstin Strandell (1997) defined the children's perspective as being concerned with:

> both taking the child's standpoint and listening to children from their position as children, and as an adult, imagining how children think in an effort to reduce the distance between the generations, which can hinder communication. (p19, author's translation)

Thus, the child's perspective must ultimately be defined as the adult's attempt to understand, often through imagination, the thoughts and views children have of their own life. On a cultural-political level, the Danish *Børneråd* has actively sought out the child's perspective by establishing a panel, made up of sixty fifth-grade classes with 1,225 children (aged about 11). In the period from 1998 to 2000, these children directly informed the *Børneråd* about their experiences, meanings and suggestions concerning topics related to children's everyday life (Hviid, 2000). Earlier in 1994, thousands of children wrote letters to the Minister for Social Affairs, telling her their views on issues that concerned them (Heering, 1996). Children often described their family problems, and the Børneråd and the Minister corresponded with the children, giving them assurances that their voices had been heard. One positive outcome was the fact that the Børneråd implemented initiatives to reduce victimisation in school. Such initiatives, where the children were visited to draw attention to their behaviour, have had a practical effect on children's lives.

These examples represent children's active involvement in a living democracy. The response of the Børneråd and the Minister for Social Affairs reflect the extent to which children's active participation is truly valued and respected.

Recognition of the child

Societal and educational values concerned with listening to children and letting them have a say are also supported by the idea of recognition, which during the last decades has had a big impact on Danish early childhood education. According to the German philosopher, Axel Honneth (1995), without recognition the individual cannot develop a personal identity; it is a precondition for the individual's self-realisation, for a good life. For that reason, a democratic society has to offer citizens a fundamental recognition, expressed via three spheres and forms of recognitions, namely: love, rights and solidarity (Honneth, 1995).

In the private sphere, symmetrical relations such as love and friendship contribute towards the development of a basic self-confidence, a kind of emotional recognition. In early childhood education and care, attachment theories are used to elaborate this dimension. The Norwegian scholar, Berit Bae (2005), applies the concept of recognition to preschool practice. Emotional recognition leads to a secure attachment, basic confidence and, with that, physical integrity.

In the sphere of legal relations, individuals may use their legal universal rights, for example, freedom of expression as an active member of society, to foster self-respect and self-esteem. In preschool, this is seen when the child uses his or her legal rights to be seen and heard, to participate and influence. When such rights are realised, the individual gets a social integrity.

In the sphere of community of value, in what can usefully be described as cultural, political and working communities, individuals strive to become integrated members of a community with a shared sense of solidarity. When the subject is recognised as a special person, self-esteem will come into existence. In preschool such communities are seen in children's play, in their mutual relations and in their shared exploration of the world. Here, children obtain a form of 'honour' dignity (Honneth, 1995:129). In contrast, when a child is expelled from the community, when he again and again hears, 'you are not allowed to take part', he loses his self-esteem.

Adults and children have fundamental needs for recognition on all three levels: emotional attention, legal and social recognition. If individuals do not receive recognition, they will be at risk of failing to develop a positive view of themselves. The ideas outlined above are now taken forward through consideration of a case study of a family in Copenhagen.

A family in Copenhagen

Many, though not all children in Denmark are involved in the daily life in their family, crèche, preschool and school, where they are seen as active and independent individuals with their own ideas and wishes. A range of significant adults, such as parents and teachers, are willing to listen to and give them the opportunity to have their say, and thus a feeling of recognition.

These developments will be illustrated by studying a specific family in Copenhagen, focusing on 5-year-old Oskar, who lives in the quarter of Øresund, situated between Copenhagen city and the airport. Oskar's father is a librarian at a Technical University and his mother works at a travel agency. Oskar has an 8-year-old brother Sebastian who attends grade 2 in the local school. They live in a city house with a shared yard where the children play and the families often meet together.

Family life is busy. Both parents have long working days and both pairs of grandparents pick up Oskar and his brother Sebastian twice a week from pre-school and a local leisure-time centre. Thus both children are accustomed to daily communication about each family member's daily experiences and are proactively involved in decisions. Thus family life is built on the ideas of democratic participation by all its members. In addition they all visit the nearby culture centre *Amager Bio* to watch theatre, film and participate in different workshops. Decision making can sometimes be problematic, when for example family members have different expectations about the best way to spend their leisure time. In order to resolve potential conflicts, importance is placed on openness, listening and the valuing of all family members' views. Conflicts do still develop, for example between sports fixtures and family events, or when the two boys' play sessions arranged with friends clash with the parents' wishes. However, the ideal for such family communication is non-compelling action, in other words, the parents try to make use of the Habermas (1994) idea of communicative action.

Oskar's life in preschool

In preschool the teachers see Oskar and his friends as individuals with the necessary level of competence to be involved in conversations, dialogues and decisions. Each day they hold both organised and open periods. The organised periods involve structured group activities where teachers and children focus on shared topics, for example, dance, song, drawing or literacy. The open periods call for children to be directly involved with their friends in decision making through the use of shared activities.

Oskar is a member of the group *the longest legs* containing all 5-year-old children, who will start school next year. During the year they decide on, and explore a range of themes and problems. In deciding on the themes, both teachers' and children's voices are heard. The issues and problems arise out of the interaction between the children and their teachers. An example of this process is illustrated below. A teacher observed Oskar and another boy's dialogue during lunch. When Oskar started to eat his bread with sausage, a boy from another ethnic background than Danish said:

'Ugh this food is unclean, why do you eat such food? My father says this is really unappetising'

Quickly Oskar replied:

'Don't speak about my food.'

And then he turned to a boy on his left side saying:

'I like this, me and my father eats this at home with roasted onion, ah, goody!'

The boys continued the dialogue and then it ran out. However, based on this situation the teacher suggested for the group of *the longest legs* the theme 'me and my family', thus giving the children the opportunity to explore each others' culture, norms and values and reflect on matters concerned with nationalism, east-west conflict etc. It is important to note how the teacher proactively uses the dialogue generated by the children and in doing so recognises and respects the individual contributions made to shape the project. This kind of activity can help to make the world transparent for the children, as outlined by Klafki (1998) and Giroux (1988).

In another example, Oskar and two friends suggested that they play and find out more about the card games Gormitti and Pokemon. As the idea came directly from the children it allowed them to lead the planning process. The activity was used to explore three questions:

What do we already know about the theme or problem?

What do we need to find out?

How can we collect new information and improve existing knowledge and skills?

In response to the three questions, Oskar suggested to the group that they take a bus to a museum he had visited together with his grandparents. The exhibition was 'Magna Japanese Pictures, Louisiana Modern Art Museum' (www.louisiana.dk).

I saw lots of pictures, cartoon books, figures and also a film, and then my grandfather asks me to hurry up although there was much more to look at.

In answer to the first and second questions, Oskar and his friends were able to use their existing knowledge about the game. They used drawings to help them express their views. In response to the third question, one child suggested they invite her big brother to visit them and show his collection. These examples illustrate how children can use their own themes and problems to influence and shape learning.

Involvement in societal changes

Over time, Oskar and his family have spent many hours in the local culture house with other participants, producing individual drawings, stories etc. The adult users of the house saw great potential in the children's creative and active participation and expression, and decided to work politically for the establishment of a children's culture house. In order to support the idea, the adults involved children directly in the development process. Thus Oskar, and specially his older brother Sebastian, became actively involved and engaged in the project *The Future Children's Culture House at Amager – when children get a voice* (www.kulturhus.kk.dk/bornekulturhus-amar). In order to let the children's ideas and wishes inform the project from the beginning, the architect invited a large group of children to participate in four workshops (twenty hours in all). The children expressed their creative ideas, produced models and explained all the details to the architect who in the first instance acted as a listener but then questioned the children further as part of the overall democratic process.

Issues raised and their current relevance

These examples show how families, preschools and local institutions can take a child's perspective and, by doing so, encourage the direct participation of children. They demonstrate that children can be involved in different aspects of their lives (Honneth, 1995). In the family and preschool (the private sphere), Oskar is involved in symmetrical relations, which give him a basic self-confidence. Furthermore, his active use of his right to express ideas (sphere of legal relations), both in preschool and in the culture house, make him and his brother active members of society (sphere of community of value). During their participation in the planning sessions for the future children's culture house, they become important members of the community, sharing with adults the development of a specific vision that is likely to increase feelings of self-respect and self-esteem.

When families, institutions and society as a whole learn to take a child's perspective and view children as competent and contributing members of a democratic society, this has the potential to produce a more open society. When children are accustomed to having a say and being involved in cultural changes, it becomes natural for them to act in ways we refer to as political. Thus, when terms like children's perspective, participation and active influence on the surroundings become fundamental words in education for all kinds of teachers, and also are integrated into new pedagogical theories, it may be possible to integrate a radical democratic perspective in society. Such a perspective is oriented towards the future and has a global perspective. It views the democratic person as a political subject with knowledge and skills and, moreover, with a desire to make use of this to transform society.

Points for discussion

- Some families challenge their children and help them to be active participants, to learn to have influence and act as democrats; other families have neither the tradition nor energy for such an approach. Will this result in more societal inequality and, if so, how?

- To what extent is it possible in the family, preschool, and first years in school to develop an educational approach promoting a child perspective, giving the child a voice and active influence?

References

Bae, B (2005) Troubling the identity of a researcher. Methodological and ethical questions in co-operating with teacher-carers in Norway. *Contemporary Issues in Early Childhood*, 6(3) p283-291

Brannen, J and O'Brien, M (1995). Review easy childhood and sociological gaze: paradigm and paradoxes. *Sociology,* 29(4) p729-37

Daginstitutionsloven (2007) Passed by the Danish Government 24 May 2007

Giroux, H (1988). *Teachers as Intellectuals: towards a critical pedagogy of learning.* Massachusetts: Bergin and Garvey Publishers

Habermas, J (1994) *The Theory of Communicative Action: reason and the rationalization of society.* Boston: Beacon

Heering, K (1996). *Sæt ord på dit liv: Børn skriver til Socialministeren om deres ønsker, meninger og drømme om et godt liv* [Describe your life. Letters from children to the Minister of Social Affairs]. Copenhagen: Børnerådet

Honneth, A (1995) *The Struggle for Recognition. The moral grammar of social conflicts.* Cambridge: Polity Press

Hviid, P (2000). *Børnepanel: På sporet af 5. klasse* [Children's panel: Following grade 5]. Copenhagen: Børnerådet

James, A, Jenks, C and Prout, A (1998) *Theorizing Childhood.* Cambridge: Polity Press

Jensen, B B and Schnack, K (1997) The action competence approach in environment education. *Environment Education Research,* 3(2) p163-178

Klafki, W (1998) Characteristics of critical-constructive didaktik. In Gundem, B B and Hopmann, S (eds) *Didaktik and/or Curriculum. An International Dialogue. American University Studies.* New York: Peter Lang

Qvarsell, B (2003). Barns perspektiv och mänskliga rättigheter: Godhetsmaximering eller kunskabsbilding? [Child's perspective and human rights]. In Johansson, E. and Pramling Samuelsson, I. (eds) *Pædagogisk forskning i Sverige.Barns perspektiv och barnperspektiv. Göteborg Universitet,* 8(1-2) p101-113

Strandell, K (1997) *Jeg är glad att jag gick på dagis: Fyrti ungdomar ser tilbaka på sin uppväkst* [I am happy for my days in preschool]. Stockholm: HLS Förlag

Trevarthen, C (1998) The concept and foundation of infant inter-subjectivity. In Bråten, S (ed.) *Inter-subjective Communication and Emotion in Early Ontogeny.* Cambridge: Cambridge University Press

Website United Nations (1989) *Conventions of the rights of the child.* www.CRIN.org accessed November 2004

16

Issues for the Present and Issues for the Future

Margaret M Clark and Stanley Tucker

Introduction

> Over the time of writing this book, during a year characterised by terrible natural and man-made disasters, millions of the world's children have witnessed or been touched by events too traumatic for most of us even to imagine. These have run alongside the day-to-day difficulties of life for some, and parallel to the joys of life for others. (Smidt, 2006:132)

This quotation from Smidt could equally apply to the early lives of the children described in this book. When, in her introduction, she considers child development, Smidt asks which child, and what development. She illustrates her point with contrasting case studies of young children from Mexico, Vietnam and South Africa. She considers different portrayals of childhood, claiming that we need an image of a child to work with, and that, for her, the child is engaged from birth in building a relationship with the world, that the child is competent and active, critical and, she says, 'challenging'. This view is in marked contrast to those who would argue that the young child is dependent, subordinate and incompetent and leads to very different portrayals of the role of adults, the curricula in the early years, and the importance of listening to the voice of the child.

Now that you have read the preceding Chapters, to what extent would you envisage the young child as competent, active and critical?

In what ways are history and culture important to an understanding of child development?

The issues covered in this book were grouped under five section headings: changes and transitions; the changing nature of social isolation; changing generations; who cares and challenges and changes. There are many other ways in which we could have considered the issues. In this Chapter we highlight some of these, drawing on specific Chapters to illuminate the points.

Our first section was headed 'changes and transitions' but many of the families discussed in later Chapters also faced repeated transitions. Transition is a common theme in books on the early years but frequently the focus is on vertical transitions that children encounter from early education through primary and into secondary school. In, for example, *Informing Transitions in the Early Years: research policy and practice* the editors point out that:

> At a time when young children are likely to have experienced many different transitions, both educationally and in their family lives, there is an increasing emphasis on an earlier start in group day care and educational settings than ever before. By the time children enter statutory education they may have already attended a number of educational settings. Each of these experiences is likely to affect children and their capacity to adjust and to learn. (Dunlop and Fabian, 2007 pxiii)

It is important to bear in mind the frequency with which many young children, well before 8 years of age, have had to adjust even within a single day to transitions, not only vertical but also horizontal transitions, These might entail changes from parental supervision, to care by grandparents or others in the extended family, child minders or baby sitters, from playgroup to nursery class. The culture and ethos may differ hugely between the various settings.

We have not dealt specifically so far with changes in policy and practice in early education and care and the new transitions faced by young children as a consequence. In the Chapters on Northern Ireland and Romania (Chapters 9 and 10) generational changes faced by families in a time of political and curricular change were explored. In this final Chapter we devote a section to a consideration of policy and practice in early education and care as it is changing in the countries from which we have drawn our examples. We also widen the discussion with reference to recent research in other countries.

Cultural background and its impact on family life

Aspects of their environment dictated family life for some of our families. Did they live in an urban or rural area, and did they face poverty? Much of the research on poverty and disadvantaged families focuses on urban areas (such as those described in Chapters 12 and 13). In Chapter 5 the isolation faced by families living in a remote rural area is discussed and the problems for the various agencies attempting to provide for the young children. In two Chapters (Chapter 7 and Chapter 8) the families discussed were not only living in rural areas, and in poverty, but were also faced with the pandemic of HIV/AIDS.

It is worth contrasting the problems for families living in poverty in rural areas with those of families living in urban areas and what the implications are for policy makers and practitioners caring for young children (for information see Chapters 5, 7, 8, 9, 12 and 13).

There are many cultural aspects that constrain or widen the experiences of young children, and these differ across the world. Children may also face changes in the culture within which they spend their early years, often following trauma, even becoming refugees, more or less welcomed in the receiving country. Some of the changes may be as strange and disturbing for the parents as for the children

In several of the Chapters, the families on which we focus have had to move to a very different culture from that of their parents and grandparents (Chapters 3, 4 and 11). Although we have not dealt specifically with the issue of children whose mother tongue and home language is different from that of the community in which they are living, this is clearly an additional feature of the lives of the New Londoners, the refugee children starting school in the Republic of Ireland and the Somali family in USA (Chapters 3, 4 and 11).

Family dynamics

Many different family structures are covered in the case studies. In some, the young children's early years are in a nuclear family with two parents and possibly younger and older siblings. In Chapter 15, the voice of the young children plays an important part in decision making in family, school and community life. In Chapter 14, on technologies in the homes of preschool children, we see the views of the parents influencing the extent to which the young children become familiar with a range of new technology. However, the children's own preferences also play a part, as we see from examples of differences between siblings in their preferences for and familiarity with new technologies.

In some of the case studies, the mother has to bear the whole burden of the upbringing of the young children, either because of the father working away from home (as in Chapter 8), the fact that the mother's admission that she was HIV positive status had led to her husband divorcing her (Chapter 7), or because the family has had to flee and they are now refugees in a very different cultural setting (such as in Chapters 3 and 11). In Chapter 3, we see the stresses where initially the mother bears the whole burden of settling the refugee family in a strange country, but is subsequently joined by the father, necessitating yet other adjustments for both the parents and the children. In one of the families described in Chapter 13, supported by the interdisciplinary team, the father is encouraged and enabled to retain an interest in the children's upbringing even after he has left the family home.

The role of siblings in the lives of young children is considered in Chapter 4 where the New Londoners are helped to adjust to life in London by grandparents and siblings. In Chapter 8, Angel faces her own traumas, but also has to face the death of her grandmother, then later of her sister and the necessity to incorporate her sister's children into her already overburdened life. In the Chapter on 'Brothers and sisters' (Jalongo and Dragich in Jalongo, 2008), it is suggested that siblings can play many different roles in the lives of young children, as rivals who vie for attention, as 'culture brokers', supporters of their brothers' and sisters' cognitive, social and cultural development, and not least as family members who adapt to special needs or even help the family to cope with sibling loss.

Many families living in poverty are large (see Chapters 9 and 12 for example). In Chapter 6 the focus is on children who are developmentally different and the social isolation they may face in preschool settings unless there is positive intervention by members of staff. Some of the other families have at least one sibling who has special needs, either epileptic or autistic; the impact of this on families already copying with major problems is severe. The problems of children who are on antiviral drugs with the stigma attached to that, and for siblings who feel neglected because they are not, are discussed in Chapter 8.

We have not considered the effect of step families on the lives of young children specifically in any of the Chapters, although that is clearly an issue for many young children who may not only have to face the loss of their father, but also the intrusion of a step father, and possibly half and step brothers and sisters (see Chapters 8 and 13). Children may start life as only children and then become one of an extended family, with both siblings and step brothers and sisters. They may suffer bereavement. According to a recent UNICEF report quoted by Simao:

> Women in poor nations were 300 times more likely to die in childbirth or from pregnancy-related complications than those in the developed world and chil-

dren were almost 14 times more likely to die during the first month of life. (Simao, 2009)

The children whose early lives we have described in the preceding Chapters illustrate the impact of traumatic change. One of the striking differences which we have not dealt with specifically is the role of gender in the perception of young children's role and what constraints their sex places on society's expectations of them as they grow towards adulthood.

It would be valuable to return to the preceding Chapters and, where the child described is a girl, consider in what ways the experience might have been different had the child been a boy and vice versa (Chapters 4, 5, 8, and 15 in particular).

The children whose early lives are described in Chapters 12 and 13 came from families with many problems, and contrasting solutions are described in the two Chapters. Because of the inability of the parents to cope, the children described in Chapter 12 were absorbed or even adopted within the extended family, or transferred to foster parents. For these particular children the outcome was positive, but for many such children their lack of contact with the extended family, time in children's homes, repeated changes of foster parents, and even return to their biological parents temporarily or permanently, may have a much less favourable prognosis. One has to consider the impact on family life for the many other children (around fifty of them) fostered in that same family for short or longer periods and, bear in mind the effect on the biological family of such conflicting loyalties, a neglected area for research. Thanks to intervention by a multidisciplinary team, the families described in Chapter 13 were able to remain as a unit, and at least in the short term; the outlook not only for the children, but also for their parents was promising. It is important to note the crucial role played by the various professionals involved, including the nursery school staff.

Many questions are being raised currently as to whether we try too hard to fix families and for too long; whether the rights of the biological parents take priority over the rights of the children. Some professionals argue for earlier adoption, many deploring the number of foster homes experienced by some of the most vulnerable young children. Some claim, in contrast, that if help were offered earlier, with parenting skills for example, it might be possible to stabilise families and avoid breakdown. There are many issues to be considered, not least balancing the risk of physical or mental abuse to the children, were they to remain in the biological family or step family, against the costs of taking the children into care (see *Working with Children in Care*, Petrie *et al*, 2006).

Grandparents are an important source of help, advice and support to many young children and their families. In late 1800s in many larger families there were still children at home when the eldest child gave birth to their first child, so there was often overlapping of the parent and grandparent roles. Now, in the twenty-first century, with greater life expectancy many grandparents live long enough not only to see their grandchildren grow up but are expected to take an active role in their upbringing. In *Enduring Bonds*, a Chapter is devoted to grandparents and redefining their roles and responsibilities (Nicholson and Zeece in Jalongo, 2008). That book is a valuable source of historical research drawn from different cultural backgrounds. It is claimed that research shows that, 'Being exposed to a nurturing grandparent in early childhood increases the chance that an individual will become an engaged grandparent in adulthood' (p134). Changes in the family structure may result from the death of grandparents who have been playing a vital role in supporting the young children. The authors remind us of the trauma inflicted by divorce not only on the immediate family but also on grandparents.

While grandparents may provide support or material assistance following divorce, in many cases there may be a disruption of the bonds between grandparents and grandchildren, and only infrequent and casual visits. In only four of the case studies in this book is the role of grandparents specifically referred to: in Chapter 4 the grandparents played an important role in the lives of the New Londoners, bridging the two cultures for the children, often with the assistance of siblings. In Chapter 8 Angel's life was happy while she was supported in her chores by her grandmother, but things changed dramatically on her grandmother's death. In Chapter 9, one grandfather, who had lived through The Troubles in Northern Ireland and who was still bitter was likely to have coloured the family's views of life, even after the end of conflict.

Some of the children we have discussed no longer have any contact with their grandparents, for example, the refugee families discussed in Chapter 3 and the Somali family in Chapter 11. In several of the case studies, grandparents were faced with the challenge of raising some of their grandchildren. It has been reported recently that: 'Almost two-fifths of grandparent carers live below the poverty line and are struggling to cope, according to research from Grandparents Plus' (*Children's Services Weekly*, 30 October 2009:4).

For those families discussed in Chapters 7 and 8, not only was there poverty and isolation but also the effects of illness, in particular the pandemic of HIV/ AIDS, and bereavement. Some children, even at a very young age, have to adopt adult roles or, as referred to in Chapter 8, have to develop some degree of 'adultification', owing to changed family circumstances. Such issues are, however, not confined to countries such as Malawi and South Africa. Young children who are faced with taking on the role of carer because of the long-term physical or mental problems of their parents, or because the parents are neglectful, also face many types of deprivation, and they also have to adopt an adult role at an early age.

Consider the differences between the childhoods of the children who feature in the case studies in Chapters 5, 7 and 8 and list the most important features causing these differences.

Policy and practice in early education and care

It was never the intention here to discuss in detail the policies underpinning early years education and care; the ways these are changing the early lives of young children well before they enter statutory education; the changes in the expectations placed on parents and their role in their children's upbringing. In this section we guide you to references to enable you to develop an understanding of the different aims, policies, practices and curricular developments in different parts of the world from which we have drawn the case studies. We also suggest references that deal with more general policy issues and research in other parts of the world. Many of the children upon whose early life we have reported have attended a variety of provision in their early years; furthermore, depending on where they live, the age at which they have entered primary school will have varied greatly (from 4 to 7 years of age). In several of the Chapters there is some discussion of the preschool provision in that country (two contrasting examples are Chapter 2 Iceland and Chapter 7 Malawi and local team provision in Glasgow in Chapter 13).

Early years policy can be described as a social construct, because its nature and content are dependent on the social and cultural context within which it is framed and implemented; this will vary widely from country to country and over the years. Two recent publications that have as their focus developments in policy are *Understanding Early Years Policy* (Baldock *et al*, 2009) and *An Introduction to Early Childhood* (Waller, 2009), in Chapter 5 of which Waller considers 'International perspectives'. Baldock stresses the impact of policy decisions by central and local government on the daily lives of practitioners as well as the families for whom they provide, determining as they do both the level of resources and the way these must be spent. It is questioned whether increased provision is appropriate for all; whether the curriculum offered meets the needs of individual children and whether there is support in place to meet the diverse needs of each child.

The families discussed in seven of the Chapters in this book live in the United Kingdom or, in the case of Chapter 3: the Republic of Ireland, Chapters 4 (England), 5 (Wales), 9 (Northern Ireland), 12 (England), 13 and 14 (Scotland). Following devolution, the policy and practice in education and care differs greatly in the constituent parts of the United Kingdom, and the gap is widening. *Early Childhood Education and Care: policy and practice* (Clark and Waller, 2007) is a valuable source of information on these developments. Each of the five Chapters in that book is preceded by two case studies reporting on the early years experiences of children born in 2000. Although none of these ten children had by the age of 7 moved to a different part of the United Kingdom, yet they had experienced many changes, even disruptions to their family life. It is worth comparing these children with those whose early experiences are highlighted in this book, who have been selected to illustrate specific types of experience.

It would he valuable for you to develop your own case studies to share with others, perhaps tracing the early experiences of a child born in 2005. This will help to bring alive the impact of new policies on the lives of young children.

Chapters 2 (Iceland) and 15 (Denmark) describe the experiences of families from two of the five Nordic countries (Denmark, Finland, Iceland, Norway and Sweden). Einarsdottir in Chapter 2 provides a clear outline of the policy in early years settings in Iceland and the other Nordic countries which she contrasts with other policies. Chapter 2 showa how different are the views on early education in Iceland, and indeed the other Nordic countries, from those in many countries where the focus is on school readiness. In the Nordic countries, the focus is on play and encouraging social relations, an approach fully endorsed by the parents. Chapter 15 reveals yet another feature of early education in the Nordic countries, namely the importance given to the voices of young children in decision making in the family, preschool and community (see *Nordic Childhoods and Early Education*, Einarsdottir and Wagner, 2006).

Starting Strong II: early childhood education and care (OECD, 2006) is a valuable review of developments in early childhood education and care across the twenty participating countries. It contains information relevant to Chapter 6 (Australia), Chapter 15 (Denmark) and Chapter 11 (the United States) as these were among the participating countries. Important policy issues are also discussed there, including social and economic policies and their impact on early years education and care, women's labour market participation and reconciling work and family responsibilities on a more equitable basis for women. Other topics explored are how countries approach such issues as diversity, the impact of child poverty and educational disadvantage, and are influenced by their social and economic traditions.

In Chapter 6, social isolation is discussed, in particular of children who are either gifted or have developmental problems, in an Australian preschool centre. We see how these are resolved by the staff and with the help of some of the other children. Further information on this and other issues with particular reference to Australia are to be found in *Children, Families and Communities* (Bowes and Grace, 2009).

One final publication to widen your horizons on global issues related to early childhood policy and practice is *Preschool in Three Cultures Revisited: China, Japan and the United States* (Tobin *et al*, 2009). An interesting technique was adopted in this research whereby the researchers made videos in a particular preschool in each country. The videotape was edited to be used as the focus for discussion by professionals, parents and other groups in that country and in the other participating countries. The authors report on the changes they found on revisiting the three preschools involved in their previous research in 1980s where the authors now made a further video. They also sought the current views of the professionals on seeing again the earlier video some years later. A further preschool was selected in each country where they collected video evidence as a basis for discussion.

We have three very different cultures represented in this research and this technique enables us to look across time and cultures and determine how much life in preschools has changed over the past twenty years. Although the impact of political, economic, and demographic changes on each country's early childhood education over the past twenty years is revealed, the central concern of the research is with culture, what is retained and what is modified with new policies and approaches. Tobin and his co-authors consider the changes across time and cultures; they argue that preschools in China, Japan and the US have changed in some ways and stayed the same in others:

> but we cannot say that they have become better or worse, just that they each now, as a generation ago, reflect their culture, their society, and their time. (p247)

The same is no doubt true of the communities in which the children whose lives are discussed in this book are growing up.

References

Baldock, P, Fitzgerald, D and Kay, J (2009) *Understanding Early Years Policy.* Second Edition. London: Sage

Bowes, J and Grace, R (eds) (2009) *Children, Families and Communities: contexts and consequences.* Third edition. South Melbourne, Victoria: Oxford University Press

Children's Services Weekly (2009) Two-fifths of grandparent carers live below the poverty line. 30 October p4. Crediton, Devon: The Education Publishing Company

Clark, M M and Waller, T (eds) (2007) *Early Childhood Education and Care: policy and practice.* London: Sage

Dunlop, A-W and Fabian, H (eds) (2007) *Informing Transitions in the Early Years: research, policy and practice.* Maidenhead: Open University Press

Einarsdottir, J and Wagner, J T (eds) (2006) *Nordic Childhoods and Early Education.* Greenwich, Connecticut: Information Age Publishing

Jalongo, M R (ed) (2008) *Enduring Bonds: the significance of interpersonal relationships in young children's lives.* New York: Springer

Jalongo, M R and Dragich, D (2008) Brothers and sisters: the influence of sibling relationships on young children's development. In Jalongo, M R (ed) *Enduring Bonds: the significance of interpersonal relationships in young children's lives.* New York: Springer

Nicholson, L and Zeece, P D (2008) Grandparents in the lives of young children: redefining roles and responsibilities. In Jalongo, M R (ed) *Enduring Bonds: the significance of interpersonal relationships in young children's lives.* New York: Springer

Organisation for Economic Co-operation and Development (OECD) (2006) *Starting Strong II: early childhood education and care.* Paris: OECD

Petrie, P, Boddy, J, Cameron, C, Wigfall, V and Antonia, S (2006) *Working with Children in Care: European perspectives.* Maidenhead: Open University Press

Simao, P (2009) Urgent action needed to cut maternal deaths: UNICEF. http://www.reuters.com/articlePrint?article=USTRE50E3H620090115 Accessed November 2009

Smidt, S (2006) *The Developing Child in the 21st Century: a global perspective on child development.* London: Routledge

Tobin, J, Hsueh, Y and Karasawa, M (2009) *Preschool in Three Cultures Revisited: China, Japan and the United States.* Chicago: University of Chicago Press

Waller T (ed) (2009) *An Introduction to Early Childhood.* Second Edition, London: Sage

Index